Contents

Introduction

By Jay Morrison

The Bengals were coming off a 2-14 record that was tied for the worst in franchise history and had missed the playoffs in five consecutive seasons when they drafted Joe Burrow in 2020. Season ticket sales had plummeted to an all-time low, while acrimony among the fan base, not to mention the Greater Cincinnati population in general, soared.

The team hadn't won a playoff game in more than 30 years. Owner and team president Mike Brown was still viewed with contempt by many after threatening to move the team out of Cincinnati before becoming the recipient of what the Wall Street Journal labeled "the worst stadium deal ever struck by a local government."

With that sweetheart lease set to expire in 2026, there was a growing sentiment around town to just let the franchise leave.

The Bengals needed Burrow to save them.

Everyone else pleaded for the Bengals not to ruin Burrow. The Ohio native and former Ohio State Buckeye had just compiled the greatest season in college football history to win the Heisman Trophy and a national championship at LSU.

Fans watched his rookie season with a mix of awe and angst as Burrow suffered blow after blow behind an inexperienced and inept offensive line. He ultimately suffered a devastating hit that shredded his left knee 10 games into his career.

But Burrow was back on the field six months later for the first practice of OTAs. Last November, one day shy of the one-year anniversary of the ACL tear, he guided the Bengals to a 32-13 victory in Las Vegas to kick start a run that would lead the once woebegone franchise to an AFC North Division title, their first playoff win in more than three decades.

The following week at the team hotel in Nashville, the night before that Divisional Round game against the Titans, Burrow delivered an impassioned speech demanding the players drop the "Why Not Us?" mantra, insisting they were not underdogs but rather a damn good team.

Burrow, who had played through a throat contusion and was still feeling the effects of a dislocated pinky suffered in December, got sacked a playoff-record nine times before hitting Ja'Marr Chase for a 19-yard gain with 15 seconds to go to get the Bengals in position for the game-winning field goal.

Upwards of 15,000 Bengals fans traveled to Kansas City the following week for the AFC Championship game. Burrow led his team back from an 18-point deficit for a 27-24 overtime victory and berth in Super Bowl LVI, where the team came within 85 seconds of their first championship.

Burrow not only made being a Bengals fan fun again. He made it cool.

A team that didn't even have a pizza sponsor in 2021 suddenly has a wave of interest from corporations wanting on board the Burrow train, including three marquee title sponsors who are aligning with the franchise for the first time.

But Burrow's impact goes way beyond how those on the outside view the Bengals. It's changing how the Bengals view themselves and how they do business. It's something players, agents, coaches and politicians have been trying and failing to do for years.

The northernmost franchise without an indoor facility is building one. And a front office that has never spent big on interior offensive linemen dropped $53 million combined on Alex Cappa and Ted Karras this offseason with input from Burrow, who said he doesn't view pressure off the edge to be nearly as problematic as a defensive push up the middle.

And a large portion of the "never give the Bengals another dime of public money" crowd suddenly is in the "do whatever it takes" camp after Cincinnati City Council outlined a plan to make nearly $500 million in upgrades to Paul Brown Stadium, or whatever it is to be called next.

Calling Burrow a game-changer feels woefully inadequate. He has the potential to alter the entire landscape of the city and the future of the franchise. ▬▬

THE ORIGINS OF JOEY FRANCHISE

Becoming Joe Burrow

How LSU's Reflective Leader Found His Voice After Making a Cross-Country Gamble

By Brody Miller

JULY 19, 2019

A few days before Joe Burrow made the biggest decision of his life, he needed to get away from the noise. There were the coaches, the media reports, the back-and-forth in his own mind about where he wanted to spend the final two years of his college football career. He needed to escape. He told his father, Jimmy — himself the defensive coordinator at Ohio University at the time — he needed two days not to talk to anybody.

"OK, I'll make sure all the coaches know: no phone calls for the next 48 hours," Jimmy agreed.

Burrow interrupted him.

"No, Dad," he said. "That means you and Mom, too."

Burrow was an Ohio State graduate transfer leaving after a close quarterback competition with future first-round NFL Draft pick Dwayne Haskins. The way the process worked for Burrow he would wake up one day thinking he wanted to go one place and wake up the next thinking another. One day it would be LSU. Then it might be Cincinnati. The goal was to have the same thought for four consecutive days. That's when he would know for sure, "because I think if you wake up one day and say 'Oh, I'm gonna go here,' the next day you might regret your decision after you made it," he reflects back now.

And that's just how Joe Burrow is. He thinks about things. He keeps thinking about them. He thinks about whether he is or isn't doing the proper amount of thinking. He's somebody who publicly debates NCAA student-athletes' rights on Twitter, opines about black holes — and white holes? — and asked at Fiesta Bowl media day, "Who wins in a fight: a lion or a gorilla?"

So to make the biggest decision thus far in his life in May 2018 — LSU or Cincinnati — Burrow spent two days with his Ohio State friends and roommates in Columbus, Ohio. He didn't lock himself in a room or anything. He simply removed himself from the decision and spent time with friends doing things they normally do.

Burrow came out of that 48 hours with his mind made up. His goal growing up was never about playing in the NFL like most young quarterbacks. "My goal had always been to win a national championship being the quarterback of the high-profile team."

He chose LSU. And in the past 14 months, Burrow has become a Fiesta Bowl winner, a team leader and one of the top returning quarterbacks in the SEC.

But that's not all he's learned since leaving home for Baton Rouge.

———————— 𝔸 ————————

Joe Burrow's clothes weren't drying. Every time he'd attempt to do laundry at his new one-bedroom Baton Rouge apartment, it would take forever for the clothes to dry. "What's going on here?" he began to wonder.

Then Jimmy Burrow came down to visit his son and was informed of the issue at hand. He immediately pulled out the dryer lint trap and showed Joe it was full of lint. Burrow had no idea he had to clean it out.

"So this is very embarrassing, but I had never done laundry before moving to Louisiana," Burrow admitted Monday. "So, yeah, quick dive into my insecurities."

He'd never truly been on his own. Burrow grew up in Athens, Ohio, then went to school just 70 miles northwest at Ohio State. Jimmy and Robin could drive up to get dinner with him whenever they wanted, or even just for a quick trip to get an ice cream cone. "I did that several times,"

Robin said. He didn't know how to cook much. He didn't know how to take care of his car. His mom did his laundry.

And there is the first way people will tell you Burrow has grown in the past year. He can do more on his own now, his parents think. "Yeah, independent, baby," Burrow says now of his newfound laundry skills.

Cooking, for example, has become a passion. He likes making chicken, rice, peppers, mushrooms and broccoli together and mixing them. That's his favorite. In the morning he makes omelets with turkey bacon and a bagel (he's trying to get up to 220 pounds before the season). He makes steak, salmon, tilapia and spaghetti. There's still trial and error, though. The other night he burned a chicken quesadilla, but it was his last tortilla, so he had to eat it.

"It was pretty gross," he said. "Yeah, it was black."

Burrow arrived in town last summer and dove into a four-man quarterback competition at LSU with Justin McMillan, Lowell Narcisse and Myles Brennan. He tried to keep his head down and work the first month or so. He didn't want to be the transfer coming in too confident, so he quietly studied how the team interacted before opening up. He impressed teammates during the conditioning test — finishing up front when coaches said he wasn't expected to participate right away — but there was still the awkward dynamics of an already established quarterback room.

McMillan was a popular player, and he was the front-runner coming out of spring practice before Burrow joined the team. The quarterback room itself was amicable, with both Burrow and McMillan calling each other friends, but there was some team tension when McMillan transferred midway through August camp and eventually landed at Tulane. A sizeable faction of the team thought McMillan deserved the job, and instead, McMillan and Narcisse both left and Burrow became LSU's starting quarterback.

Soon came a players-only meeting to sort through team issues. Player after player stood up and expressed their thoughts. LSU players like John Battle and Jacob Phillips said at the time it was about whether they'd divide or stay together.

Then Burrow stood up.

"If anyone has anything against me or anything to say, let's get it out on the table right now," multiple people in the room recall Burrow saying, "because I'm here to win and I'm here to lead the team."

The team was surprised. He hadn't spoken up much all camp. Former LSU walk-on quarterback Andre Sale was one of those people in the room.

"At that point, everyone was like, 'He's ready for this,'" Sale said.

In April, Joe Burrow entered Standard Hall bar in Columbus' Short North neighborhood following Ohio State's spring game. A year ago, he was in town still trying to win the Buckeyes' quarterback competition. On this day, he was a Fiesta Bowl-winning LSU quarterback who threw for nearly 3,000 yards and ran for more than 500 yards for the Tigers.

The bar erupted when he entered, old friends hugging him and reminiscing. Ohio is still home for Burrow, and these people are still some of the closest in his life. He keeps in touch with most of his Buckeyes teammates, as well as the Ohio State staff. He was in Nashville later that month for the NFL Draft to celebrate with Nick Bosa when the defensive end was selected No. 2 overall by the San Francisco 49ers. He acknowledges he became emotional after seeing viral videos of Ohio State teammates and fans — in Arlington, Texas, to face TCU — cheering for him after they showed Burrow leading LSU to a comeback win against Auburn on the AT&T Stadium video board.

That was the most difficult part for Burrow, leaving the Ohio State community and all his teammates to go play for another school.

In a time of constant transfers and debate about whether it's good or bad for college football, the perception is sometimes that a quarterback doesn't want to compete when he leaves a school. People often think somebody transfers because they want handouts. Many times, that's the case.

He's asked whether that perception ever gets in his head. He acknowledges he hears those rumblings.

"Let me think about that for a second," Burrow said, looking off to contemplate how he feels.

He often says he chose LSU specifically because he wanted to compete. Most people close to the situation say former Ohio State coach Urban Meyer never actually gave the job to Haskins before Burrow left. Burrow and Jimmy discussed a transfer that January, but Burrow decided to stay to continue competing all spring. When he did announce he was transferring, at least five SEC schools courted him, Jimmy said, but Burrow liked LSU, Cincinnati and North Carolina best.

"The reason ultimately he ended up in the SEC was when you're at Ohio State and at the top of the college football world, then you go to LSU and the SEC, it's the same," Jimmy Burrow said. "You have to prove yourself in the best conference in college football, and that was part of his mindset going into it."

It took time for Burrow to win over the LSU team, and he entered a flawed offense that struggled in pass protection and lacked efficiency. They kept winning, though. LSU started 5-0, beat No. 2 Georgia, finished 10-3 and won a Fiesta Bowl as Burrow found his stride down the stretch as one of the better dual-threat quarterbacks in the SEC.

He developed a reputation for taking hits, usually fighting for extra yards on runs instead of sliding or going out of bounds. For much of the season, Burrow was the only healthy scholarship quarterback while Myles Brennan dealt with a back injury. Still, Burrow didn't protect himself. "I do believe that Joe, if we let him, would run into a brick wall no matter what it took," Ed Orgeron said Monday. Sale was the backup when Brennan was hurt, and he jokes now about how he never got to play because Burrow shrugged off every major hit. The only times he actually came close were the three instances when Burrow — who wore older cleats from the late 2000s — had to get his laces replaced mid-game.

He's the son of a former Nebraska defensive back and longtime defensive coordinator in Jimmy. He's the youngest brother of Jamie and Dan, former Nebraska linebackers and safeties, themselves. Being physical is in the Burrow family's blood. He was a physical defensive back in his Athens High School days — he likes to brag about being a double-digit-tackle-a-game kind of DB — and he used to beg Meyer to let him play kickoff.

He's always been physical and competitive, but the change Jimmy and Robin see most in him is his competitiveness. They now see him getting chippy with defenders when he takes hits or yelling to the crowd after touchdowns.

The wake-up call for them was when Burrow ran straight into the center of a pregame scuffle before the season opener with Miami in Arlington, Texas. He hadn't played a snap for LSU yet, and he was in the middle of the commotion, shouting back at Hurricanes players.

"I was like, 'Whoa! Who is that?'" Robin said. "I've never seen him like that."

——————— A ———————

Twice a week this summer, Burrow and some other LSU leaders organize players-only seven-on-seven practices for the skill players. LSU has a new passing game coordinator in former New Orleans Saints assistant Joe Brady, a 29-year-old rising star bringing in a new offense built on run-pass options and a modern passing system.

And here's the next change you'll find in Joe Burrow: He's now the guy, along with senior linebacker Michael Divinity, leading their respective sides of the ball, planning practices and hyping the team up.

"It's night and day for me," Burrow said. "I knew probably 10 people's name on the team when I was here at this point last year."

The timing of Brady's new passing game comes at an opportune time, as well. Burrow is now the veteran presence who feels comfortable running the show. Brady raves about how Burrow learns things in seconds, and Burrow takes pride in then teaching it to the younger guys. One staffer said Burrow acts like an extra coach.

Brady and offensive coordinator Steve Ensminger always ask Burrow what he likes and doesn't like, and the senior gives them feedback on what things LSU should or shouldn't run, in his opinion. They listen to him.

"Joe Burrow is everything you want in a quarterback," Brady said. "If you give me 11 Joe Burrows, we're going to be a winning football team. Having Joe behind center you have a chance to win every single game. He makes everyone around him better."

Brad Kragthorpe was an LSU offensive analyst when Burrow arrived and left in February for a job with the Cincinnati Bengals. The biggest change he saw by the time he left?

"It's his team," Kragthorpe said. "Joe Burrow is the dude in that building now."

——————— A ———————

Some things don't change much, though, for Burrow. He doesn't take any classes on campus, as the liberal arts master's program only requires online classes, so he'll be in the quarterback room hearing teammates discuss certain buildings and have no idea what they are talking about.

As of March, he said he still hadn't done much exploring. "I know where Perkins Rowe is. I know where Highland (Road) is, and I know where the casino is."

He spent much of last season saying he treats his two years in Baton Rouge like an internship program — he interned at Goldman Sachs one summer — so he didn't go out and party. He was focused on his game. In the spring, he was asked whether he's sticking to that plan and said with a smirk, "I mean, it's the offseason. I did my little thing at Mardi Gras."

But his final college fall camp begins in weeks, and Burrow spent Monday at SEC media days displaying the two ends of how he has and hasn't changed in the past 14 months. He's still the quirky, off-the-wall thinker who loves constructively debating sensitive topics and wearing funny socks, but now he's the established SEC quarterback leading a team with College Football Playoff hopes. Geographically, personally, athletically, he's in a different place from where he was in the spring of 2018.

So how has Joe Burrow changed most in the past 14 months? Some will say he's more independent. Others will say he's more of a leader. One might say he's more comfortable.

Then it becomes Burrow's turn. He's asked directly, "How do you think you've changed most in the past 14 months?"

He leans back in curiosity and rubs his fingers on his chin, thinking about it for several moments. He can't just answer with a generality. That's not who Joe Burrow is. He's trying really hard to figure out the right answer.

"Honestly, I don't know," he says, leaning forward now. "That's kind of a deep question that you're just throwing on me and trying to get me to answer in 30 seconds. That's something I think you need to take a week to reflect on, kind of. I'll think about that."

He gives up.

"Ask me about that at camp."

So how has Joe Burrow grown in the past year? How has the Ohio quarterback progressed on and off the field as LSU goes into a season with some of the highest expectations in years?

We'll find out this fall, in more ways than one. ▬▬

Hometown Legend

How Joe Burrow, LSU's Heisman favorite, Rose to Prominence in Athens, Ohio

By Jon Greenberg

DECEMBER 5, 2019

Tell people from Athens you want to talk about Joe Burrow, and all you need is one question and some time.

Where were you when LSU went into Tuscaloosa and rolled the Tide?

Trae Williams, a defensive back at Northwestern, was in Evanston, Illinois, having just lost the eighth game of his disappointing fifth-year senior season.

"I'm sitting there with my roommates, and obviously those are some of my best friends, and they were cheering for him like they know him too," said Williams, an Athens High classmate of Burrow. "That's just how we are, like, that's my boy, so that's their boy too."

The Luehrman twins, Adam and Ryan, having played a game on Wednesday, were there in Athens. First, at an Ohio University football practice, where a trainer dispatched first-half updates, including Burrow's two touchdown passes and LSU's six scoring drives.

They hurried back to their apartment to watch the second half with another former teammate from Athens High to celebrate LSU's 46-41 victory.

Ryan Adams and Nate White, who coached Joe Burrow at Athens High, were at their respective homes for the entire game.

"There were several people around town that had parties," White said. "But I really enjoyed just my wife and me on our small couch taking it all in. I loved watching it very closely without any distractions."

Zacciah Saltzman, whose Georgetown football career ended early because of injuries, was on the scene, sitting in the at Bryant-Denny Stadium stands in Tuscaloosa with Burrow's older brothers Jamie and Dan, and their parents, Jimmy and Robin. Saltzman was on the receiving end of Burrow's passes at Athens, but still was slack-jawed at witnessing his former QB going 31-of-39 for 393 yards and three scores with no interceptions.

"I was like, 'Man, who does this against 'Bama?'" Saltzman said.

For family and friends, Burrow's ascension to Heisman favorite and potential top draft pick makes perfect sense. Yet, as Burrow stands on the precipice of leading LSU to a SEC title and possible national championship, just how his career has fallen into place seems inexplicable.

"I'm not a guy who goes to church every Sunday," Adams said recently from his office off of the Athens Middle School gym. "I don't say this to everyone. But it's almost divine intervention."

Whether at Tony's Tavern, Ohio University's E.W. Scripps School of Journalism or the halls of the middle school, people are talking about the community's favorite son. They put up marquee signs, like the ones at Gigi's Diner and a drive-thru liquor store; and they plant purple-and-gold flags in front of their houses.

The local Walmart now sells LSU gear. That's a detail that Joe's friends love to share.

"How nuts is that?" Saltzman said.

Athens is a postcard college town in the heart of a very poor part of Appalachia. The scenery is beautiful, from foliage in Wayne National Forest to the gorge and waterfalls of Old Man's Cave. But southeast Ohio has poverty rates more than twice the national average, and Athens County is the most impoverished in the state, with 31.2 percent of residents living below the poverty line.

In the center of this struggling region sits Ohio University, which employs 4,125 residents, more than the county's next 14 employers combined. The 20,000 students who rotate in and out of town nearly outnumber the 24,000 townsfolk. This mix of stable university jobs amid economic strife, of transient students living among generations of families, creates a unique community.

"It's really tough to explain Athens," Saltzman said. "I talked to Trae about this because he goes to another very wealthy high academic school, and there's really no way for people to understand what it was like growing up in Athens. I just tell them we're from a small town and leave it at that. But it was a cool place to grow up."

Adams, a native of the area, has become a bit of an amateur sociologist, watching how kids interact as they negotiate their early teenage years.

"It's an interesting dynamic, how some kids can relate across the board, and other ones kind of stay in their safe zone," he said. "From the time that Joey came in here, in regular phys-ed class, he had a way to cross all those different boundaries. And even more, he was very sympathetic to those that weren't as athletically gifted or affluent. He had a little bit of a soft spot for those guys and would always pick them to be on his team."

Like any gym teacher worth their whistle, Adams likes to keep teams even. But when they did three-on-three basketball, Burrow asked to choose his team.

"He picked two kids that are probably the least athletic in his class," Adams said. "Well, they win every game."

So the next game, Adams changed the rules. Burrow couldn't score two baskets in a row.

"He's tossing the ball off," Adams said. "Nobody sets picks in middle school. He's setting picks, this, that and the other. They clean house, right? They win every game."

Adams smiled as he recalled this story, clear as day almost a decade later. The next time Burrow's team played, he wasn't allowed to score at all.

"And, by God, he got those two kids to play their butts off," he said. "And he's setting screens and giving them little cherry-pick shots off each side of the basket. They won every game."

This year's LSU squad has just one other player from Ohio. Last year's had none. Burrow came into a proud program without much of a college reputation. He was an Ohio guy who didn't win a job at Ohio State and now had to transfer. Knowing this, Saltzman said he was curious to learn how Burrow won over his new team in Baton Rouge.

"It's interesting hearing about how he went into a big-time program like that and established himself as a leader. How do you do that?" Saltzman said. "He won every sprint over the summer and then people see, 'Oh, you're tough,' and then he can start to give them his personality and then become friends.

"He's great at that stuff. When you go to the NFL, how do you go to a new locker room and be the guy? And that's something I think he's super natural with."

The house on the outskirts of Athens is on a quiet, well-kept street that would fit into any American suburb. A small LSU flag is planted next to a faded Ohio one in the front yard. A football wreath and a purple LSU banner adorn the door.

Many coaches at Ohio University live in The Plains, a few miles north of town and campus. The Burrows settled here when Jimmy got the defensive coordinator job under Frank Solich in 2005, toting along their elementary school son. It's important to remember Burrow isn't just some local kid gifted with a big arm, a predestined gift from the football gods. No, Burrow was bred for this. Wherever he lived, from Iowa to Nebraska to North Dakota to Ohio — he was going to prosper.

"He grew up in it," Solich said. "He grew up in that kind of atmosphere."

The Burrows are a college football family. Jimmy, a Mississippi native, played in the mid-70s at Nebraska as Johnny Rodgers won a Heisman. His two older sons (Joe's half-brothers) played football at Nebraska too, and Jimmy coached there for two years when Joe was just four and five years old. There should be a picture, somewhere, of a young Joe and 2001 Heisman winner Eric Crouch, Jimmy said, he just has to look for it.

"He's got football in his blood," Williams said. "His brothers were really good athletes. His dad was. Grandparents were. He's just got it in him, and he really eats, sleeps, breathes it."

What was a young Joe Burrow like? Were the signs there?

"I remember thinking this is just an intense little kid," Saltzman said. "He was just super-serious and he had a mentality that was a lot different from the little guys running around playing basketball."

"He was competitive," Jimmy Burrow said. "You know, when you're not supposed to be keeping score in those early soccer games, and he would know exactly the score and you know he likes to compete and he likes to win. And I think that's OK. That's a good thing."

Athens High always has Ohio University coaches' kids suiting up, but many don't stay. They show promise as sophomores then a parent gets a new job. None, however, were as good as Joe Burrow.

Solich stayed at Ohio for 15 years, recently breaking the Mid-American Conference's record for wins. Jimmy Burrow was at his side until this year.

"My parents would tell me, 'You know Joe's dad will probably find another job,'" Ryan Luehrman said. "And eventually, he's here for the long haul."

Solich embraced a family atmosphere. If OU was on the road for a Saturday game, he would let Jimmy Burrow and defensive line coach Jesse Williams, Trae's dad, meet up with the team later so they could watch their sons play for Athens High. The mid-week "MACtion" games made it a little tougher because of the mixed-up schedule, but Burrow doesn't think he missed more than a couple of his son's games during his junior and senior seasons.

"I wasn't like a helicopter dad or you know, a taskmaster," he said. "I didn't say 'Hey, you gotta come watch this tape.' I'd say, 'Hey, I'm gonna watch your game, you wanna watch with me?' And he usually would, and I would point out little things like protecting the ball and making good decisions."

Jimmy retired after last season so he and Robin, a nearby middle school principal, could spend this year following their son at LSU. He expected to host tailgates and spend hours driving through the South, both of which he's done. What he didn't account for was the barrage of text messages.

"If I don't turn my phone off here, it's going to be crazy," he said mid-interview. "You'd realize what I'm doing these days."

The elder Burrow has become de facto spokesman for his son, and his days are packed with interviews. He does a weekly hit on a Baton Rouge radio station. Last year, he refused almost all interview requests so as not to take away attention from the Bobcats. Now, he's like a tour guide of his son's life.

"Last night it was ESPN, you're here, CBS is here in the morning," Burrow said from his kitchen. "ESPN is here again tomorrow afternoon. The Washington Post was here last week."

When Ohio played in nationally televised "MACtion" games this season, the ESPN producers asked if Jimmy would be around. He was interviewed in back-to-back games as the announcers were thrilled to talk about Joe and LSU and not, say, two MAC teams.

A shrine to the family's athletic achievements sits in the basement of the Burrow house. Jerseys are tacked up on the brown paneled walls, including Jimmy's from the Packers and the Canadian Football League and the elder Burrow boys' uniforms from Nebraska. A poster of Joe in a basketball uniform lays on the ping-pong table.

At the far end of the room near the TV and video game system are the trophies and plaques. The Ohio High School Athletic Association doesn't make a trophy for its Mr. Football award, so Jimmy made one himself, a football on a pedestal.

In the upstairs living room is Joe's Fiesta Bowl MVP trophy, one that Jimmy didn't make to order. He lugged that home from Phoenix in his backpack and let the airline workers take pictures with it. Now it sits by the fireplace.

The photographer taking pictures of him mentions she's from Cincinnati. Jimmy smiles. The Bengals are in line for the top pick in the draft. The drive from Athens to Cincinnati is a lot shorter than the drive to Baton Rouge.

Before he was Burrow's offensive coordinator, Nate White was a quarterback at Athens High in the late 1990s, when a four-win season was considered a success.

"We weren't very good at all," said White, who took over as head coach of Athens High this season.

After an uneventful career as a backup quarterback at nearby Marietta College, White got his first high school job at Tri-Valley High School in Dresden and started running a veer offense, something fairly typical in the world of Ohio prep football. But he eventually transitioned into an offense with spread concepts.

When he was hired at Athens before Burrow's sophomore year, White approached Adams about running a spread-based offense. Adams had already started tinkering with those concepts and gave him the go-ahead. It would prove fateful for Burrow, who was already progressing as a quarterback.

That summer, Burrow had led Athens' 7-on-7 team and White saw him slicing apart teams. White was building a playbook that wasn't overly complex, but it required an accurate quarterback.

"It was the middle of July and I remember saying, 'This kid is really good,'" he said.

He also had two tall receivers in the Luehrmans, another solid wideout in Saltzman and Williams, the new kid in town, in the backfield. It was an unusually talented core of players.

"We went to the state championship with two running plays," White said. "We had zone and we had quarterback trap off of zone. The rest was passing stuff."

Even the passing plays were basic. But like any good offense, the key was Athens could expertly execute just about every play out of multiple formations.

"Very rarely in high school football is everyone covered," White said. "You watch high school games, there's always someone open but it takes a special kid to always find the guy.

"In practice, I'd say why didn't you throw it to this? Joe would essentially say, I don't know this well enough yet. We've got to talk. We'd stop right there and fix it. Just the poise and confidence to say, 'I don't know this well enough. I don't want to do anything else until I get this.' As a 15-, 16-year-old kid, that's so rare."

Burrow threw for 4,437 yards and 63 touchdowns his senior year. His 11,428 passing yards are the fourth-highest in Ohio history, and his 156 touchdowns are the third-highest, behind the famous (in Ohio football circles anyway) Mauk brothers, Maty and Ben.

In 2014, Athens High scored a state-record 861 points, 57.4 a game, just 4 points shy of the school's 22-3 basketball team. Yes, Burrow led that team in scoring with 19.3 points per game.

They beat Wellston 82-7 and followed that up with a 77-14 win against River Valley. They scored more than 60 points in a game six times, putting up 66 on the road in Zanesville. Their home games had a circus-like atmosphere, Saltzman said, and opponents were beaten before taking the field.

"I remember there were legit teams where these kids would put Sharpies in their socks, so when we're in the handshake lines at the end of the games, Joe could sign their gloves and stuff," Saltzman said. "I was like, this is absurd."

"We were always kind of chasing the perfect game, where we'd score every drive and complete every ball," White said. "It sounds crazy to say, but that was really the way he prepared and it rubbed off on everybody."

Did it ever happen?

"We had a few where we scored every possession," he said.

Williams, who played running back at Athens, could only remember one time when his quarterback was flustered. It came during a playoff game their senior season.

"The only time he'd ever been confused on what signal our coach was giving, I got confused," Williams said. "I was like, Joe doesn't know, then maybe I don't know," Williams said. "And the coach was freaking out, 'Why aren't you all running the play?'

"And Joe was like, 'Dude, I don't know what he's talking about.' I said, all right, I'm going to run a little swing and just throw it to me. He snaps the ball, looks at me, and then runs 70 yards for a touchdown."

The ball would've been fine in Williams' hands. His father was a well-traveled college assistant coach who had landed in Athens for Trae's sophomore year. Fast and strong, Trae was a natural fit in White's offense at running back and ran for 5,435 yards and 96 touchdowns in three years at Athens.

"If you called inside zone, Trae Williams was 70 yards and gone," White said. "That might have happened 40 times in three years. He made calling plays easy. Just call 'zone' and he might score."

Williams committed to Ohio as a running back, but backed out to attend Northwestern as a defensive back. Solich thought he had Williams, and he made sure the Bobcats were first to offer Burrow.

"Obviously it became clear that he was going to head to a Power 5 program and that Ohio State was very interested in him," Solich said in his office recently. "And we understood his decision. So we were patting him on the back and following his career from that point on.

"If Ohio State hadn't made an offer," Jimmy Burrow said, "we still thought maybe he would have chosen Ohio, as opposed to a lot of the Power 5 schools. Just because he loved the Bobcats so much."

Athens High lost Burrow's first game as a starter when he was a sophomore, but then won every regular-season game heading into his senior season. Granted, the competition wasn't stiff in the Tri-

Valley Conference, and when Athens faced better teams, it had lost in the regional finals in 2012 and 2013. That left the team feeling as if it had something to prove in 2014.

"Before the year, Joe and Trae called everyone together," Adam Luehrman said.

"I remember Joe was like what's our goal for this season," Ryan Luehrman said. "And I said regional championship. He asked, 'Why not further?' And I was silent. You got me there. Yeah. Why are we limiting ourselves?"

Adams had already set up a test that would push his team. That spring, he got a call from Reno Saccoccia, coach of the Steubenville High Big Red, who was looking for a midseason opponent. If Adams's team wanted a challenge, here it was: In the previous 10 seasons, Steubenville had a record of 115-16 and two state titles. The school was also embroiled in the aftermath of a sexual assault by two football players in 2012, a case that became a touchstone across the country and that cast the community's legendary rabid support of football in a different light.

Athens knew that Harding Stadium at night would not be an easy environment.

"Steubenville was a measuring stick for us," Saltzman said. "Let's see if we're the real deal. We've been playing in southeast Ohio killing people, let's go play an historic program and show all of Ohio what we're made of."

Steubenville is an old steel town along the Ohio River, about three hours from Athens. If you followed the Athens team bus north, you'd drive the Lou "The Toe" Groza highway through Martins Ferry, the focus of the poem that opens up the Pulitzer Prize-winning book, Friday Night Lights.

Athens needed this win for more than just street cred. A weighted playoff points system and Athens' weak conference made running the table the only certain path to the playoffs. The Athens players remember the atmosphere when they arrived at Steubenville's packed stadium: a loud marching band, home fans overflowing into the visiting bleachers and a fire-breathing horse sitting atop the scoreboard.

"For a high school stadium, what an intimidating place to play," White said. "I remember (aside) from the 40 to the other 40 on our visiting side were home fans. It was not ideal."

"I realized exactly what we were stepping ourselves into when we got to Steubenville," Adams said of a key detail left out of his conversations with Saccoccia. "It was homecoming. But apparently Coach Reno also didn't realize what I was bringing on the bus."

Despite a few uncharacteristic mistakes, Athens led 29-27 at halftime, helped in part by two long scores: a 70-yard zone run up the middle by Williams and a 48-yard sideline catch and tightrope act by Ryan Luehrman. With rain about to pour, Adams felt like he needed to fire up his team in the visiting locker room.

"I paced a lot, like all coaches do," Adams said. "And, I went back outside to check conditions one last time. And, the rain was blowing horizontally, I mean, it was 20-, 30-mile-an-hour winds. And I said, 'Boys, you know, if you've ever wanted any more adversity, man. You have got it. It is all here tonight.'"

What was his speech like? Memorable, even five years later.

"At halftime," Saltzman said, "I was sitting next to Joe and Trae, and Coach Adams is like 'All right boys, we gotta do this for coal country. We're from coal country and they're from steel country. We've got to show them what's up with the coal guys.' And we're getting hyped up and Trae looks at me and Joe looks at me and we're like, 'Hey, wait a minute, we don't come from coal mining families. But we're still going to do this shit.' We were going crazy, like 'We have to do this for the coal miners!'"

Athens still led by two going into the fourth quarter, then scored 22 unanswered points as Burrow threw a 43-yard touchdown to Adam Luerhman before scoring on a 48-yard keeper to seal a 58-42 win. In the crucible of his high school career, Burrow threw for 360 yards and four touchdowns and ran for 83 yards and two more scores.

"I don't know if it was Joe's best night numbers-wise," White said, "but it was probably his most dominant performance in high school."

Dmitri Collaros, now a second baseman at Division III Otterbein University, was the Big Red quarterback that night. He knows a pro quarterback when he sees one (his older brother Zach won the 2019 Grey Cup as the starter for Winnipeg), and was amazed at not just the throws he saw from Burrow, but the elusiveness, the toughness. He saw defensive linemen and linebackers bounce off Burrow when he ran the ball. On one fourth-quarter carry, it took a gang of five Big Red defenders to stop Burrow's forward progress 20 yards downfield. They never brought him down.

Five years later, Collaros jokes that he was a cocky high schooler and when they watched tape of Burrow before the game, he told teammates, "I'm better than this guy."

He wanted to believe it, too. Even after the game, he jokingly repeated his bluff, until one of his coaches called him out.

"He said, 'Can you take a three-step drop and throw a 15-yard out to the opposite hash mark?'" Collaros recalled. "I said, 'No.'"

How many high school quarterbacks can?

———————— A ————————

No matter what happens this December in New York City, there will likely never be a person who has been named Mr. Football, Gatorade Player of the Year, Heisman Trophy winner and Gridiron Glory Player of the Year.

Why?

Because Burrow never won the Gridiron Glory award. Not as a sophomore or a junior (when he won his first Gatorade award) or even as a senior, when he was named the best player in the entire football-crazy state.

Gridiron Glory is a weekly TV show put on by broadcasting students at Ohio University. It's a staple of southeast Ohio football.

But the player of the year award was, until 2015, voted on solely by fans, and as Karli Bell, a former student who worked on the show in 2014, explained, fans of other schools would vote more often than ones in Athens. That's how Hunter Sexton, the quarterback of Jackson High, beat Burrow for this award his senior year.

In fact, Burrow wasn't even up for the award because the Gridiron Glory staff oddly nominated the whole Athens offense. Sexton, who put up around 1,500 combined yards compared to Burrow's 5,000 or so, is now a relief pitcher at Marshall. And, yes, he gets a kick out of beating Burrow for the award. So do his friends.

"They joke about it," Sexton said. "They ask why I didn't end up playing football in college."
Sexton's team at Jackson was no joke, though. Two of his teammates that year went to Division I schools after Jackson went 10-0 in the regular season and won a playoff game.

"We were the two top teams in that part of the state," he said. "Just to see that sort of talent and know he was going to OSU. It's kind of awesome I ended up winning."

While his friends joke that he could've won the Heisman, Sexton appreciates the differences between him and Burrow as teenage quarterbacks.

"I mean, honestly, you could tell he was on another level," Sexton said, echoing a refrain you hear from practically every quarterback who had to match up against Burrow.

Athens had to come back from a 17-7 halftime deficit against two-time defending state champ St. Vincent-St. Mary to make it to the 2014 state championship game. SVSM quarterback Dom Davis looks back and remembers how calm Burrow and Athens remained coming out for the third quarter.

"You had that feeling of impending doom coming out of halftime," he said. "Maybe we just pissed him off. The second half was all him. It was a one-man wrecking crew."

Davis said during the game he stood on the sideline waiting for Burrow to make a mistake, to throw off his back foot into coverage, something. But even when Burrow did make a play under duress, Davis remembers him putting the ball where only his receiver could catch it. Burrow would pick apart a defense with quick slants, screens and hitches "and then all of a sudden, they throw a 30-yard bomb and it would be a completed pass."

Athens won, 34-31.

"It's an hour bus ride home," Davis said. "And I was thinking that dude will end up winning the Heisman and be the first pick of the draft. I thought he was that good."

Now, five years later, he watches LSU games like everyone else, appreciating what he saw then, what he sees now and whether he's going to prove prophetic.

"I played against Joe freaking Burrow," he said.

—————————— A ——————————

The eye test favored perennial football power Toledo Central Catholic in the 2014 state championship game.

"The biggest thing I remember pregame is looking at their team and our team and getting the vibe that everyone in the stadium thinks this is not going to go well," White said. "It kind of looked different."

The Division III state championship game was at Ohio Stadium. Burrow had verbally committed to the Buckeyes the spring of his junior year, but signing day was months away. So the recruiting was still ongoing.

"It was very cold," Jimmy Burrow said. "(Ohio State's offensive coordinator) Tom Herman sat with us during the game and we had to give him a blanket."

A little more than 10,000 people filled Ohio Stadium that day, and Athens had a sizable contingent, and not just from the town. On the bus ride out of southeast Ohio, Burrow and his teammates saw rivals rally in support.

"Logan High School put up a banner on the overpass on Rt. 33 going up to Columbus," Ryan Luehrman said. "It was amazing, there was a whole convoy of fire trucks."

In a show of solidarity, Sexton, still basking in his Gridiron Glory, showed up in Columbus with his Jackson teammates. They weren't alone. It felt like all of southeast Ohio was following Athens High.

"Football in Athens historically hadn't been very popular," Adam Luehrman said. "But I remember the state championship game, there were so many rows of people, alums in their old varsity jackets, it was a sea of gold and green."

On the field, the game was as advertised, a shootout between two teams of distinct styles. State

championship records fell. Toledo Central Catholic old-schooled its way to 501 rushing yards. Athens threw for 446 yards and six touchdowns.

According to the game story in the Columbus Dispatch, only two second-half possessions didn't result in points, including Burrow's second interception of the season. But Toledo Central Catholic had the last opportunity and scored an 8-yard touchdown run with 15 seconds left for a 56-52 win.

"That game is such a blur now," Ryan Luehrman said. "Those last few plays, those were the slowest seconds of my life. It was a heartbreaker. It took me a long time to quit replaying it in my head."

"I still haven't watched it," Adam Luehrman said. "I watched plays when I did my highlight reel, but I haven't watched the final plays yet."

Adams said he was nervous about what his players would say in a press conference after the game. But they handled it well. As Jimmy Burrow recalls, his son said, "it's the worst day of his life."

"Coach (Urban) Meyer, on our official visit, which might've been like a week or two later, said that the most impressive thing about the whole game was Joe's interview after the game," Jimmy Burrow said. "He had watched the press conference and he thought Joe handled it the way you would want someone to handle it."

—————————— ——————————

Burrow signed with Ohio State the following winter. He redshirted, excelling off the field in Columbus and in the weight room, but when it came time to earn a starting job, a hand injury in August 2017 hurt his chances. Before his redshirt junior year, with a degree already in hand, he would be eligible immediately if he decided to transfer.

When it came time to choose, Jimmy said OU came up again, but considering that the Bobcats had a solid returning starter in Nathan Rourke, the coach in him didn't feel comfortable pushing it. And Ohio didn't really fit with Joe's vision. He wanted to win a national championship, not a MAC title.

That he chose LSU over Cincinnati was a bit of a surprise, though, given the Tigers' longtime infatuation with the run. But Ed Orgeron promised they'd open up the passing game, which he did this season with the addition of passing guru Joe Brady.

"Rarely is Joe is overly excited," White said of Burrow. "But this summer he was drawing stuff on board to show me what they're doing. 'We're going to throw it around and be one back or empty.' He was very confident they were going to change."

LSU becoming a high-octane passing team is about as shocking as Athens High going to the state championship. In 13 games last season, Burrow threw for just 2,894 yards, 16 touchdowns and five interceptions.

On Nov. 30, through 12 games, Burrow set the SEC single-season record for passing (4,336 yards), tied the mark for passing touchdowns (44) and still threw only six picks. His accuracy has been even more impressive than his totals — his completion percentage has shot from 58.7 percent in 2018 to a nation-leading 78.3 percent this fall.

"It literally looks like high school football in the SEC, which is bananas," said Saltzman, who attended a number of games in person this season. "This guy is literally throwing the same completion percentage in the SEC as he did in high school against the TVC. It's hilarious."

Crazy as this seems, are the people who knew him then surprised by the heights he's reached now? No, not really.

"He's a genius," said Williams, who texts regularly with Burrow and his other Athens teammates. "He knows everything. These are the same things that I've seen him do when I was literally right there beside him."

"I remember the first summer I came to Georgetown," Saltzman said. "It was Joe's redshirt freshman year at Ohio State, and we were talking about good people we played with. My friends from New Jersey played against guys like Jabrill Peppers. I was like, 'You know what guys, I'll tell you what right now, the quarterback I played with is going to win the Heisman before it's all said and done.' They were like 'Nah, no shot, who is this kid?' I was like 'Just wait on it.'"

Had Burrow succeeded like this at Ohio State, the results would've seemed more in line with all of those expectations like Saltzman's. But in some ways, Burrow dominating at a place like LSU makes it even sweeter.

"It's still absolutely a pinch yourself, can't believe it's happening kind of deal," White said.

"It's been a complete joy for me," Adams said. "I've had all the time in the world to really just bask in these games."

Whenever Burrow comes back to Athens, Ryan Luehrman said they mostly lay low at the twins' apartment. When they don't, like when they went to a high school road game last season, Burrow is hit with a barrage of selfie requests.

Burrow will never be just a kid from Athens again. As the stars align, the demands will only grow. A Heisman, the postseason, the NFL draft. Even after his first season at LSU, when he started all 13 games, he still lived a relatively normal life by college football standards.

"I went down to Baton Rouge over the summer," Saltzman said, 'and we were driving around and Joe's like, 'Man, I'm in Louisiana. How about that?' Yeah, I never would've thought. This is pretty crazy."

Solich has seen it all. He succeeded legendary Tom Osborne at Nebraska and won a Big 12 title two years later and averaged nine wins in six years. The fan base still turned. When he first got to Athens in 2002, he said there were OSU flags everywhere. But they were eventually replaced by OU ones as his program started winning every year. He knows that fan bases are rarely built overnight, which makes those LSU flags around town all the more remarkable. Which is why next fall, those LSU flags will likely be replaced. Perhaps by Bengals flags.

But before Burrow thinks about the NFL, he has unfinished business. The key to Burrow's decisions to both attend Ohio State and transfer to LSU were predicated on the chance to win a national championship. Now Burrow's two schools, his past and his present, are first and second in the college football playoff rankings. And if Burrow ends up playing the Buckeyes for a national title?

"If that happens," Adams said. "Every goddamn one of the stars aligned." ▬▬

'What Are the Odds of That?'

Inside Joe Burrow's Heisman Trophy Weekend and the Coronation of a Reluctant Star

By Brody Miller

DECEMBER 15, 2019

The best college football player in America stands in the heart of a rainy Times Square waiting to see a billboard of his own face. He doesn't want to do it. No, Joe Burrow hates these things. But 29 hours before he takes home the Heisman Trophy, Burrow has to be the center of the sports media world.

ESPN's Holly Rowe is pre-recording interviews for the ceremony. For Burrow, she wants to do it in front of the large Times Square billboard LSU purchased to promote the LSU quarterback with the flashing words "Burrow" and "Heisman." One problem: It isn't coming up.

So they wait in the New York rain for the billboard to play. Fans and random pedestrians are screaming "Joe! Joe!" as they notice who it is. Rowe and company are sure the billboard is coming. It's played non-stop for the past five days. Why would it stop?

Burrow stands, unamused, hands in the pockets of his blue, block L LSU letterman jacket, waiting to get another media obligation over with. Rowe makes small talk as they wait. Burrow forces a smile and paces back and forth, his hands never leaving his pockets. They wait for upwards of 10 to 12 minutes.

The billboard never plays. By some fluke scheduling mishap, the billboard didn't run for the one hour of the week they needed it. Rowe does the interview anyway.

A few minutes later, Burrow and his massive contingent of LSU communications staffers steering him through a long week of awards and interviews ride the elevator up to the Marriott Marquis lobby for yet another media spot. Burrow looks up from his phone and confirms he at least did see the billboard once earlier. Still, everyone frustratedly laughs at the situation.

THE HEISMAN MEMORIAL TROPHY
PRESENTED BY
THE HEISMAN TROPHY TRUST
TO

JOE BURROW
LSU

AS THE OUTSTANDING COLLEGE FOOTBALL PLAYER
IN THE UNITED STATES FOR
2019

"What are the odds of that?" asks Brandon Berrio, LSU's associate director of creative and digital content.

Everybody shakes their heads.

"Well, about the same as Joe winning the Heisman."

— A —

Burrow won the Heisman Trophy on Saturday night. An LSU quarterback, of all positions, took home the most prestigious award in college football. He did it by the biggest landslide in the award's 85-year history. He did it in New York with 59 people from LSU in attendance to see it, plus his parents, siblings, cousins and so on.

By now, the story of Burrow is known: How he transferred from Ohio State to the bayou in 2018, became LSU's starting quarterback, led the Tigers to a 10-3 Fiesta Bowl season despite a middling performance, returned for his senior year and became the best offensive player in school history. How he led LSU to a 13-0 start this season, its first win against Alabama in eight years, an SEC title and the No. 1 seed in the College Football Playoff while seemingly breaking every major passing record in SEC history.

And Burrow has spent the entire season saying the only goal was a national championship. He downplayed nearly every question about accolades and records. He kicked the Heisman topic down the road every week he could. "That's something to worry about later," he'd say.

But this is not a story about Burrow, his path and what he's accomplished. This is a story about the Heisman no longer being something to worry about later. It's about the Heisman finally being here. It's about two days in New York, the whirlwind week that took Burrow away from football and how a normally stoic football guy finally broke down emotionally on national television.

This is the story of Burrow's Heisman weekend.

— A —

Thirty hours until his name is announced, Burrow enters Marriott Marquis Broadway Lounge, hands in his pockets, gliding toward a sea of media members set up at four tables ready to ask him questions he's already been answering for weeks. He's wearing the LSU letterman jacket, jeans, white sneakers and his hair set up with that one loose curl poking out front that he claims does it on its own. By his side are the other three finalists: Oklahoma's Jalen Hurts and Ohio State's Chase Young and Justin Fields.

This may be where the story begins, but it's by no means where Burrow's week starts. He's already exhausted. On Wednesday, he was in Baltimore to receive the Johnny Unitas Golden Arm Award. On Thursday, he was in Atlanta to take home the Davey O'Brien and Maxwell awards. Friday morning, he was on a flight to New York for the most draining of them all.

"It's been a long week," Burrow says along with a sigh, "waking up early and going to these awards, but it's a blessing."

The media session is set up with four tables for four finalists. Each finalist spends five minutes at each table. Each table is a mirror image of the last, a glimpse into the media life of a high-profile athlete, the same questions asked in the same way on repeat. There are the Ohio State questions at one table. There are the transfer questions. There are the Billy Cannon questions. There are even multiple playful questions about why he always wears the same Fiesta Bowl sweatshirt everywhere. Each question receives the same answer. Table after table.

Burrow does not love participating in media functions. The problem is he's quite good at it. He gives funny answers and intriguing insights and is often engaging. But Burrow is one of those guys who simply wants to be locked in a dark film room studying tape or on the field perfecting timing with his receivers. He doesn't go out much. He jokes he only knows three locations in Baton Rouge. He has few concerns other than football, which is part of why his weekly Monday media setting was cut in half to just one combined news conference because it was all just too much for him.

Imagine him spending a whole week going city to city, interview to interview, public event to public event for four days straight. He perseveres. He knows he has no right to complain about winning awards. He may be good at it, but in brief moments, the strain in his eyes is evident.

One reporter asks Burrow how he handles the newfound fame. "It's pretty easy to deal with during the season," he says, "because you have practice every day, games on Saturday, go home, go to bed, do the same thing the next week."

By that, he means, it's tougher to deal with this week.

He gets just a short 45 minutes or so to himself Friday afternoon. He gets up to his hotel room and immediately lays down. An exhausted Burrow tells his girlfriend, Olivia Holzmacher,

"Olivia, I can't talk anymore."

The finalists move from one obligation to another, from interviews to signing footballs to recording segments for ESPN. As they ride the elevator down to the first floor, they run into 1995 Heisman winner and former Ohio State running back Eddie George.

George says a few words to each of them, and then they decide to take a picture of George with the Ohio State finalists. Burrow and Hurts move off to the side.

Then it occurs to everyone: Burrow was an Ohio State guy.

"Wait, Joe, you want in?" George asks.

Burrow and everybody around laughs. Burrow politely declines as to not interfere. The next stop is walking out to the center of Times Square with Rowe to pose for pictures with the trophy. It's around this time it begins to rain. They hold an umbrella over the trophy.

Burrow and his fellow finalists take turns talking to Rowe and waiting in the rain. Everybody in America understands Burrow is going to win, and by a landslide, so it makes for an interesting dynamic. The other three are seeming more relaxed and enjoying the trip while Burrow has a greater weight on his shoulders and more responsibilities.

It's a slow evolution of people realizing who's walking by. Eventually, people are shouting at Burrow. One guy does an impression of Ed Orgeron. They yell things like, "You've got it in the bag. Heisman's yours," and, "Good luck, Joe!" One group of four 20-something women repeatedly shouts at Burrow. None appears to be football fans. They just understand somebody famous is involved. They jokingly taunt the finalists, and when Burrow doesn't turn around, one of them says, "Oh, are you feeling yourself today?"

That gets a laugh out of Burrow. He turns around, breaks a sly grin and nods his head.

Cannon died May 20, 2018. He was LSU's only Heisman winner, taking home the trophy in 1959.

Burrow officially signed the paperwork to play football at LSU on May 20, 2018.

Cannon is the most revered player in LSU history. He's the proprietor of the legendary "Halloween Run" against Ole Miss, the man who took LSU to its first national title in 1958 and its only Heisman winner for six decades.

Burrow has gotten to know the Cannons this week. He met with Cannon's widow, Dot, on Tuesday. Then, the Cannon family wrote Burrow a letter that he read on the flight to New York. Burrow wanted to keep the contents of the letter private. He did disclose a conversation he had with Cannon's daughter, Bunnie.

"She said he would be so happy looking down on me, and that means so much to me," Burrow says. "They said he was a tough guy just like me, said we would have been best friends."

Sixty years after Cannon received the Heisman Trophy from then-Vice President Richard Nixon, Burrow sat in (more) interviews Saturday afternoon when he was asked about the significance of May 20, 2018. Does he believe there's a greater power at play making those things happen?

"I'm a kind of superstitious guy, and so there's too many things like that in football to not believe in something," Burrow says. "I don't know if you believe in God or a football God or anything like that, but there are too many things like that in life to just have coincidences like that."

Finally, Burrow could relax, at least a little. He had one brief obligation Saturday morning. Then, he was free until the ceremony. The family said he could spend the day however he pleased.

Burrow and Holzmacher stayed in. Burrow's mother, Robin, said the two ordered food to their room and did very little until Burrow had to leap back into public figure mode.

"I think I took three naps today," he says. "The last few days have been pretty exhausting."

It's been an exhausting week for nearly everyone involved. His father, Jimmy, the recently retired Ohio defensive coordinator and now de facto public relations head for the Burrow family, spent the entire day distributing tickets to the large number of family members in town for the ceremony. Even Robin joked, "It's been a long week, and we're not even the ones doing interviews."

One of the consistent threads in Burrow's interviews during the week has been whether he'd truly enjoy the moment. He always discusses having just one goal — winning a championship — and rarely leans into those sorts of things, but the two days were purely about him and his upcoming honor. How would he balance the College Football Playoff semifinal in two weeks with also attempting to be present for this weekend?

"I try to put that off until next week," he said Friday. "I'm just trying to enjoy this week right now. It's a once-in-a-lifetime experience. I can focus on that Monday when I get back."

And in the hours leading up to the ceremony, he still seemed stoic. He still seemed worn down and unsentimental.

Would Burrow really take the moment in?

The four finalists leave the final pre-ceremony interviews, hop on some escalators and head downstairs to finally walk to the PlayStation Theater for the main event. A large crowd sits at the bottom of the Marriott Marquis escalator as the players ride down. Burrow stands in front.

An Ohio State contingent begins loudly yelling, "O-H!" — "I-O!" Burrow, an Ohio native, can't help but smirk, recognizing that awaits him before the biggest achievement of his life so far.

The Heisman organizers have each player walk across the street to the theater one at a time with their family and a security detail. Burrow, the first alphabetically, goes first. Hundreds of fans yell for autographs and scream for the attention of the LSU quarterback. At one point, a confused woman turns to a friend and asks, "Is that the President?"

The Burrow clan walks up to the PlayStation Theater entrance and stops before the main hallway. A long group of fans lines both sides of the path. As they wait for the signal to walk in, Burrow and his father turn to each other. Jimmy says a little something and they both start laughing together.

Then, Burrow gets the go-ahead. He walks down the hallway and into the theater. The next time he walks through that hall, he'll be the Heisman Trophy winner.

Jamie Burrow admits the men of the Burrow family are not emotional. Jamie, Joe's eldest brother, has seen their father cry just twice in Jamie's 41 years. Joe, Jamie and Dan are the same way. They're stoic. They're tough. They do not let their emotions overtake them.

Burrow is unable to speak, grabbing his eyes, his voice squeaking as he tries to put into words the meaning of a Heisman Trophy with his name engraved on it sitting to his right. It takes him nearly 40 seconds to compose a sentence. At one point, he can only laugh at the unfamiliar feeling, a moment of complete vulnerability on the largest stage.

He needs to compose himself speaking of his hometown in Southeast Ohio. The poverty rate is nearly two times the national average. He spoke of people without food on the table. He said he's doing it for them.

He earns laughs talking about how Louisiana has taken him in, how he's "learned to love crawfish and gumbo."

But then Burrow needs his longest break to regather himself when speaking of Orgeron. His eyes get red and his voice sinks into his throat.

"You have no idea what you mean to my family," Burrow says.

As he thanks Orgeron for taking a chance on a three-year backup and handing him the keys to LSU's offense, even Orgeron turns red as he struggles to contain his tears. Jimmy, sitting next to Orgeron, has his arms around him. And right as

Burrow becomes his most emotional, he quips, "I sure hope they give him a lifetime contract. He deserves it."

After a season of downplaying it, after an exhausting week he wanted over, after his family seeing him emotional so rarely in life, Burrow broke down as he won the Heisman Trophy while giving a speech national reporters are already calling one of the best ever.

"That's the most I've cried in my 23 years of living," Burrow said later.

Burrow was raised in Ohio, but he finished growing up in Louisiana. It was at LSU where he finally learned how to cook, do laundry and service his car. It's where he finally became a starting Division I quarterback. It's where he went from an average SEC quarterback to one of the best in conference history. It's where he became the man who can give that speech, let himself feel every second of the moment and embrace one of the most important moments of his life.

And sure, he'll fly back to Baton Rouge on Sunday and begin preparing for Oklahoma. He'll try to reduce the memory and refocus on a national title. He'll go back to what he always says was the No. 1 goal.

But no matter what he does the rest of his life, Burrow will also be remembered for this night, this season, this award. He'll be "Heisman winner Joe Burrow" in most descriptions. His life will never quite be the same.

As the ceremony ended, the first thing Burrow did was take the trophy back into the heart of Times Square. He lifted it up to his chin and smiled.

In the background was a billboard. It read, "Joe Burrow: Heisman." Now, he can enjoy it. ▬▬▬

Etching a Place in History

The Night Joe Burrow Solidified His College Football Legacy

By Brody Miller

JANUARY 14, 2020

Eventually the chaos dies down and the confetti settles to the floor and the man returns to a place somewhere between his dreams and what happens when they've all come true. Ed Orgeron finishes maybe his final interview and walks with his wife Kelly across the purple-and-gold littered Superdome field and into this foreign world of vindication.

It's 1 a.m. in the Superdome. Orgeron and his LSU Tigers just won the national championship. It's all really happened. He finishes one more short interview. He takes one more quick photo. He turns and calls over to his twin sons, Cody and Parker. "Boys, I'll see you when we get back," he says. The two yell back, nod and agree. They'll hop on the bus with the team.

And it's on this quiet, nearly-empty Louisiana football field in January that the story of this LSU season begins and ends. Here stands a man, a 58-year-old Cajun catapult of passion and energy who in one generation changed the fortune of his family, the outlook of his career and the altitude of his state's football program.

It goes back to the mission James Carville often recites. It's the famed political guru's late-in-life call to action about what Louisiana needs to return to glory.

"Nobody is going to come in and save us from ourselves," he says. "It has to come from within."

It came from within. It came from a man on the bayou, the son of a telephone company worker in Lafourche Parish who shoveled shrimp, made mistakes, fell from grace, learned hard lessons and built himself back up; who failed as a head coach, built himself back up again and became a laughing stock anyway; who heard the digs at his voice and the questions of his qualifications and now leads the undefeated No. 1 football team in America.

2020
NATIONAL CHAMPIONSHIP
NATIONAL CHAMPIONSHIP
LOUISIANA STATE UNIVERSITY 2020

Orgeron is the answer to Carville's prophecy, or something like it. He's a man who saved himself when most gave up on him and who changed his ways in a profession where so few can. He saved LSU football, taking it in three seasons from a home loss to Troy and an offense in the stone age to one of the best seasons in college football history.

And as Orgeron strolls through the confetti and exits the Superdome, it still struggles to settle in. LSU did it. It won the damn thing.

"This is for everybody," Orgeron said earlier as LSU received its trophy. "One team, one heartbeat, baby."

———————— 𝔸 ————————

Joe Burrow isn't just smoking a cigar. No, he's strutting with it, head cocked back, shoulders pronounced, smoke blowing into the air above him. He's selling this. He wears a hat reading "Big Dick Joe." He's leaning into every aspect of his ever-growing legend, reclining back against a leather sofa with another puff of smoke and a subtle grin across his face.

The LSU quarterback, the Heisman Trophy winner, is the opposite story of Orgeron. He's the outsider from Ohio. He's a transfer who couldn't win the job at Ohio State now joining a school that simply couldn't develop an elite quarterback. Like Orgeron, though, he's the one now puffing a cigar with the last laugh.

See, Burrow doesn't get to be this guy often. That's how he's here in the first place. He's compulsively competitive, a hyper-focused football obsessive known for death stares at his receivers and countless hours working on timing. He's the most confident human in any room he enters. He just picks his spots when to display that.

Watch Burrow as he walks off the field during each drive Monday night. It's nearly robotic how machine-like his reactions are both good and bad.

LSU punts for an unprecedented third-straight drive. Burrow goes to the bench, sips his water twice, puts on his headset.

Burrow throws a 52-yard touchdown pass to Ja'Marr Chase to break the seal. Burrow goes to the bench, sips his water twice, puts on his headset.

Burrow takes a massive hit to the ribs on a late first-half touchdown pass, knocking the wind out of him and forcing him to bend over as he exits the field. Burrow goes to the bench, sips his water twice, puts on his headset.

And despite Clemson throwing the kitchen sink at him, despite LSU's worst start of the season and blitzes constantly confusing them up front, the magician adjusts. LSU was shocked to see Clemson play man coverage. So he slides in laser quick short passes. He dances around sacks and makes throws downfield. He takes off on designed third-and-long runs when nobody expects it.

So when Burrow knows they've sealed it, when he throws for 463 yards and five touchdowns with another rushing score to finish one of the best seasons in college history, that's when you can see the non-robotic Burrow. That's when he emphatically points at his ring finger while walking to the sideline. That's when he dances, waving his arm up and down as the LSU band finally plays "Neck."

And as Burrow's won every award and broken nearly every record, go back to Burrow sitting down at SEC Media Days in Hoover, Ala., in July.

"My goal had always been to win a national championship being the quarterback of the high-profile team," he said. "My goal growing up was never to play in the NFL. I wanted to play for — originally it was Nebraska — but it turned into somebody at this level and compete for a national title."

Burrow is officially a cigar-smoking legend now, one who will have a statue of him in Baton Rouge sooner rather than later. He's reached a place in

LSU lore that may never be matched. He's asked about his hero legacy in the state.

"What we did tonight can't be taken away from us," Burrow says. "I don't know about the whole hero thing, but I know this national championship will be remembered for a long time in Louisiana."

──────── A ────────

Eight years ago, Zach Von Rosenberg sat in this very Superdome with a drastically different perspective. He paid $1,200 a pop for two tickets to see LSU play for a national championship, a game it embarrassingly lost, 21-0, to Alabama. And in the eight years since, Von Rosenberg's minor-league baseball career ultimately failed. He joined the LSU football team. He became the 29-year-old punter who enjoys making jokes about his age and wine drinking.

That loss, that embarrassment, it sent LSU into a tailspin it seemed unable to recover from. It went on a six-year run of 8-to-10-win seasons but recruiting fell off. Character value plummeted. By the time head coach Les Miles was fired in 2016, his replacement (Orgeron) had holes to fill, obstacles to hurdle and seemingly years before any sort of title contention.

Now spot Von Rosenberg turning to the scoreboard Monday night with four minutes to go. He holds his hands behind his head, his mouth agape in disbelief. Safety Grant Delpit just knocked the ball out of Trevor Lawrence's hand. LSU recovered. LSU would win, 42-25.

"It's exactly what I wanted it to be but even better," Von Rosenberg says. "I'm speechless. It's unbelievable."

How did it all turnaround so fast? There is a long list of reasons: Recruiting, the hiring of Joe Brady, finding Burrow, etc. But as longtime LSU trainer and sports science expert Jack Marucci roams the field Monday night, he reiterates to The Athletic, "Character matters."

Marucci began a study 18 years ago that attempted to quantify character. He uses an uncomplicated metric to rate each player in the program. Nearly 20 years of evidence has made his case clear. The five highest-rated character classes all played for or won a national title. The 2017 class — Orgeron's first — is one of the highest rated.

Safety JaCoby Stevens is a member of that 2017 class. Asked what made this team different after previous years of mediocrity, he said:

"We stayed together. We were down early, and we stayed together. When we were down at our lowest, we still felt like we could win this game."

──────── A ────────

LSU passing game coordinator Joe Brady picks up his girlfriend and spins her around, banging into bodies all around them. NFL star Tyrann Mathieu introduces his son to Delpit, another famous LSU No. 7, and repeats, "He like that. He Grant Delpit." Defensive linemen like Breiden Fehoko, Glen Logan and Apu Ika are running around with massive LSU flags. Logan hangs around long after most of his teammates go inside to keep holding his flag. He doesn't want to give it up.

Odell Beckham Jr. and Jarvis Landry dance with players in the locker room. Beckham even yells "Ohio State's not here" to Cowboys running back (and former Buckeye) Ezekiel Elliott, who was across the room.

Offensive coordinator Steve Ensminger embraces his son, Steven Jr., for several minutes, tears pouring out of Steven Jr.'s face. Steven Jr. lost his wife, local sports broadcaster Carley McCord, in a plane crash Dec. 28 as she flew to watch LSU play in the Peach Bowl. The tragedy made ripples throughout the Louisiana sports community.

Steven Jr. finds himself alone scanning the field Monday night. The tears won't stop coming. "I know she's watching," he tells The Athletic. Then, describing his father bringing LSU a national championship during the toughest time of his life, he says, "It's everything."

The scene on the field Monday was one of tears and dancing and hugs and pandemonium. It wasn't as dramatic as that November albatross-shaking win at Alabama, though. No, this was a scene of pure enjoyment, not disbelief. That's been the secret to this LSU team, one that can verge on cocky because it's confident it's the best team in college football. It believes if it plays its football correctly, it should win every game. It's a reflection of a coach in Orgeron who changed his ways, learning to trust his staff and be calm with his players. He doesn't yell quite like he used to. He doesn't panic when the team is down 10 like it was Monday.

But that incessant confidence is so fascinating when you look at the makeup of this championship roster, a group of bizarre stories and misfit toys. There's the coach who failed at Ole Miss. There's the quarterback who didn't win the Ohio State job. There's the three-star running back (Clyde Edwards-Helaire) and the two-star receiver (Justin Jefferson) producing like blue-chippers. There's the 29-year-old punter. There's the team leader in center Lloyd Cushenberry who was the last-second no-name addition to his recruiting class.

"Everybody's the underdog," Von Rosenberg said. "Got an underdog coach. Joe was the underdog. We had a chip on our shoulder."

And Cushenberry, he was finally ready to speak his mind Monday. The wearer of LSU's presti-gious No. 18, Cushenberry is always the respon-sible voice, the even-tempered wise veteran. He doesn't fall into controversy.

Sitting in his locker with a satisfied smile on his face, Cushenberry enjoys proving everybody wrong who criticized his offensive line for two years. He says it with gusto.

"I read a lot," Cushenberry admits. "I see a lot on social media. So I found a Clemson article where they said we're immensely overrated. I mean, 'overrated,' what have you, we're national champs. You can't take this away from us."

Cushenberry is the last player out of the LSU lock-er room and on to the bus. The no-name No. 18 finished the job.

"How about that? National champs, man. All the doubt. All the naysayers. Can't take that away."

Joe Burrow strolls back into the LSU locker room — cigar re-lit after his press conference — with an energy of detachedness to him, as if he's in his own isolated world of enjoyment behind that grin. No reporter asking questions can put a dent in this moment.

Somebody makes a joke as he walks through about how he's rich because he's expected to be the No. 1 overall NFL draft pick this spring by the Cincinnati Bengals.

"You've gotta give me a couple weeks," he yells. "I'm still broke!"

And in the hours after the win, you can find LSU players on Bourbon Street with a drink in their hand, living this moment in its entirety. Orgeron said to Scott Van Pelt on SportsCenter he'll just go home and have a ham sandwich with Kelly.

All jokes aside, LSU now resides in territory for-eign to Orgeron and his program. It's been the team on the come up. It's been the "We're com-ing" program, as Orgeron likes to say. Suddenly it's the No. 1 team, the champion with a target on its back. It has nothing left to chase.

"The whole year we're talking about, 'We're an as-cending team. Get to the next step, the next step,'" Von Rosenberg says. "Well, we literally got to the

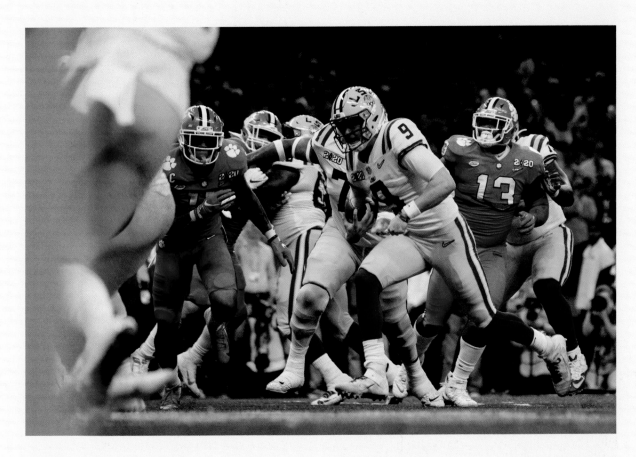

last step and won the game, and we're so used to the mentality of climbing that staircase to get to the top. Well, we're literally at the top. Nobody's gonna dethrone us."

Orgeron said on SportsCenter he'll be right back on the recruiting trail this week. Special teams coordinator Greg McMahon says "I know we're back on the road Thursday. He is relentless." Because here comes the next hurdle, the next challenge far more difficult. LSU now will try to stay at the top. It'll try to make this success sustainable. Orgeron will try to solidify himself at the top of college football.

"This is not the finish," Orgeron said. "I want to be here at LSU for a long time and to win many championships at LSU, and this is just the beginning."

But Monday night in New Orleans, a Louisiana school led by a Louisiana man went into the Superdome and etched their place in history. A man defined by his failures and flaws rewrote the focus of his biography with one night, one season, one team.

LSU football saved itself. That savior came from within. ▬▬

THE HIGHS AND LOWS OF A ROOKIE QB

The Day the Narrative Died

How Joe Burrow's Bengals Engagement Went Public

By Paul Dehner Jr.

FEBRUARY 25, 2020

From the moment the placard was switched from Notre Dame tight end Cole Kmet to LSU quarterback Joe Burrow at 8:45 a.m., the crowd of NFL media inside the Indiana Convention Center began to swell in front of podium No. 3.

As did the insistent murmurs of what could be said, has been said, anonymous perception and why the Bengals should be given the Heisman Trophy stiff arm.

The narrative fueling the sports landscape over the last month across every corner of television, radio and the internet lined up shoulder to shoulder for the latest opportunity to stir the pot.

Living up to his reputation, Burrow coolly plopped a chair down behind the microphone, the first time I've ever seen that done in nearly a decade covering the Combine.

He settled in for the long haul of what would be 15 minutes fielding questions in the spotlight.

Only one answer mattered, though. A simple yes or no question would allow reality and truth to finally overcome inferences and speculation.

I kept it direct: "If the Bengals draft you No. 1 overall, would you happily report to play for them?"

"Yes," Burrow said in a tone of near resentment at the question. "C'mon, I'm not going to not play. I'm a ballplayer. Whoever takes me, I'm going to show up."

The session could have ended there. Pack it up, everybody. See you in April.

The idea that Burrow would blow off the Bengals or "pull an Eli Manning" and refuse to sign were quashed in one word.

Only the narrative demolition didn't end there. As the words of Burrow, Bengals director of player personnel Duke Tobin and head coach Zac Taylor eventually filled the air and microphones of the expansive ballroom over the course of three hours, it became about more than killing the idea Burrow would leverage the Bengals.

It became the day the Bengals and Burrow took their engagement public.

"Of course I want to be the first pick," Burrow said. "That's every kid's dream. I've worked really, really hard for the opportunity and I'm blessed to be in this position."

Even as Burrow stated on the third question of the session that it would be special to play in Ohio, so close to his home in Athens, the attempts to push Burrow into reengaging in the narrative of trying to force a trade or belittle the Bengals came from left and right.

He was asked if he needs to hear from the Bengals to ease "concerns" about them.

"I wouldn't say there's any concerns," Burrow began, talking down the leading nature of the question. "I want to learn a lot about a lot of different teams. For these interviews, just talk ball. That's what I enjoy doing. I look forward to meeting with the Bengals here in the next couple of days. I'm looking forward to talking ball and seeing what they are about, seeing the offense that they run and see how they think about ball. So, that's what these interviews are about. Just getting to know the people and the process."

Soon after, the comment from his Davey O'Brien Award interviews, when the word "leverage" was used and spun into nearly every headline in the country, was brought up.

"I was kind of talking more about the combine process," said Burrow, who will officially meet with the Bengals on Wednesday. "So, just so everyone knows, I'm not going to throw, I'm not going to work out. So, that's kind of what I was talking about. But yeah, I'm going to try to be the best player I can be for whoever drafts me and try to fit in any way that I can."

Burrow pointed out two of his best friends from high school are Bengals fans who are thrilled at the idea of him joining their team, as would a close friend and former roommate at Ohio State, Bengals defensive end Sam Hubbard. All Burrow could do was repeatedly point out he is not the type to try to use influence over who takes him and would show up and be a team player for whatever team does.

And, oh yeah, about the narrative out there that he doesn't want to play for the Bengals? He dropped a resounding thought on that as well to hammer home the point for those not paying attention in the back.

"The only thing I've said is that I just didn't want to be presumptuous about the pick," Burrow said. "That's why I've been non-committal because I don't know what's going to happen. They might not pick me. They might fall in love with someone else. You guys (in the media) kind of took that narrative and ran with it. There has never been anything like that from my end."

The definitive nature of Burrow's answers hung in the air and the murmurs returned while the crowd dispersed following the quarterback's 15 minutes. Burrow had just taken every thought about being a problem in the draft process and picked it apart like it was Oklahoma's defense. Taylor wasn't in the room when Burrow addressed the media. He arrived for his media obligations shortly thereafter and was told of the basics from public relations director P.J. Combs.

For those not in the know with the Bengals, there was nervousness surrounding what Burrow would say. Let's be honest: He could have taken this thing sideways and caused serious consternation over the next two months.

His words, his tone, his specifics, his cool handling of the spotlight were relief.

Taylor and Tobin didn't need to hang on every word. They reacted with a shrug of an expected outcome. Privately, they've been confident about the truth inside the Burrow camp for a while.

"I didn't get to see what he said today," Tobin said when given a brief synopsis of Burrow's statement. "What our research tells us about Joe Burrow is he's his own man. He's not going to be talked into saying things for other people's benefit. If that's what he said, that's fantastic. I'm looking forward to getting to know him and getting to meet him through the process."

If you listened to the rest of more than an hour of Tobin and Taylor chatting with local reporters on Tuesday, however, you would think they have been friends with Burrow for years.

In an NFL draft game defined by being coy, dropping smoke screens and downplaying potential moves, the Bengals don't care about their poker face. They are not playing poker at all.

They are playing Uno.

"I can talk on and on about the things that he's done," said Tobin, who was a quarterback at Illinois and Colorado. "Transferring in is not easy. I'm a transfer quarterback. I know the pitfalls of that, and I know how hard it is to have a team buy into you once you get there. So, I know that firsthand. His story is such a great story of perseverance, dedication and hard work, believing in yourself and then ultimately winning at the highest level. It's a great story for everybody."

It's a better story for Taylor, who has preached the need for culture and leadership since the moment he walked in the door. He admitted after the season the Bengals still don't have enough of it. He hasn't even sat in a room with Burrow and already can tell the guy possesses everything he is looking for from that perspective.

"You see a tough kid who leads," Taylor said of watching him play. "That's something that actually stands out."

Taylor didn't care about knocks on hand size or arm strength. He sees accuracy, anticipation, decisiveness and, oh yeah, 60 touchdown passes. Even more, a presence to excel with spontaneity, a trait lacking from the offense last year under Andy Dalton.

"That is one of the great traits about him is he is able to extend plays and he has a good feel for the rush and can get out on the perimeter and those guys did a good job playing with him in that regard," Taylor said. "They threw a lot of touchdown passes that way. That's one of the things you are looking at in a quarterback: Can he create and extend plays? You don't always call the perfect call. The protection isn't always the best, so sometimes those guys have to be able to get on the perimeter and extend plays and make the play when you wouldn't think there is one to be made. That's something he's really shown on tape."

One other element of the relationship exists under the surface and came to light strengthening the public connection between the two sides.

Could the Bengals trade the top pick? Tobin didn't answer to that idea a month ago at the Senior Bowl. He did on Tuesday.

"I would say it's doubtful," Tobin said. "You never say never, but I would say it's doubtful. There are a lot of great players available to us there. You kind of know exactly what you're going to get when you start the planning process. So, I would say it's doubtful, but I never say never."

Even after one of the most definitive killings of speculation of something you'll ever see happen, the narrative, of course, would not go quietly into the rainy Indianapolis night.

An NFL Network talking head said he wouldn't be happy if he were the Bengals by what he heard, and Dan Patrick stated he didn't think it put the issue to rest.

Maybe for those not standing directly in front of Burrow as he spilled his side of things on Tuesday, they would view it a different way. So, the beat goes on it seems. Just 58 days left.

All this chatter was sluffed off as "just offseason news stories," according to Taylor and, "people have to have something to talk about and write about."

But underneath the casual dismissal, there has been a real sense of frustration from all of it. Tobin made note of it in pointing out Burrow was his own man and wouldn't let other people's agendas make him say anything.

It goes deeper than that.

Tobin found himself on Sunday still steaming over the narratives being perpetuated about a franchise to which he's dedicated the majority of his professional life.

"A manufactured narrative," said Tobin, of the idea the Bengals aren't committed to winning a Super Bowl. "I love that."

He remembers a roster he helped build to playoff appearances in five consecutive years earlier this decade and feels confident is ready to bounce back from the first year of assimilating a new coaching staff.

"The narrative isn't correct," he said. "It's not built on fact. It was built on opinion, I guess. The fact is, we're at the end of the CBA, we're trying to get a new CBA, but over the course of this past CBA,

we're a top-half-of-the-league-spending team on players. Not at the bottom. We're 13th in wins, we're top 10 in playoff appearances. Those aren't at the bottom. None of that is what we want to accomplish, but none of that says we're the worst team in the league. If we're not trying to win, let me tell you there are a lot of teams having more success doing it than us."

His feelings were made clear, but it was where Tobin opened the statement that made his point most emphatically.

"I had a lot of thoughts on that," he said. "Then I went to Mass last weekend and the gospel was Matthew. It was, 'Turn the other cheek, love your neighbor, don't wish ill will, pray for the people that want to harm you.'

"So, I would just tell a lot of the media folks I'm praying for them. I figure that (gospel) was meant for me, so I'll save some of what I was going to say."

There's not much left to say, really.

The Bengals are still going through their process, sure. They still need to check all their boxes, of course. The 15-minute interview in the suite on Wednesday and 15-minute informal sitdown with quarterbacks coach Dan Pitcher will be important, absolutely.

But Burrow said he will play for whoever takes him and wants to be the top pick. Taylor has been dying for leadership and the Bengals are positioned for their turn at the rookie-deal quarterback with that trait in spades. Tobin continues to drool over Burrow's peerless championship season, said it's doubtful he'll trade the pick and is praying for the media.

You don't need narratives to understand the situation. You don't need a career in scouting. You only need ears.

On April 23, the Bengals and Burrow will be getting married. On Tuesday, their engagement went public. ■■■■

The Zooming of Joe Burrow

Bengals Get Creative with Joe Burrow's Offseason Program

By Paul Dehner Jr.

JUNE 22, 2020

Even in a world where every day feels like a surreal alternate universe, it's hard to find much more surreal than Joe Burrow screaming cadence and audible calls to his teammates, designed for use around 65,000 fans, against the walls of his parents' house in Athens.

A few steps away is where his folks make lunch.

"It's a weird world we are living in," offensive coordinator Brian Callahan said, "but that's what it was."

What it was, more precisely, was the Zooming of Joe Burrow.

This has been the setting most days over the last month for one of the most telling and encouraging exercises in his short professional career.

Coaches were forced to carve a new path over this digital offseason teaching a rookie quarterback a system he'll be asked to master once training camp begins as he meets many of his teammates in person for the first time.

This task required creativity, imagination and impeccable Wi-Fi.

What emerged, however, is an experimental test case in how to immerse young quarterbacks in the NFL experience and a cementing of the reasons the Bengals have always been all in on Burrow.

"Everything I would have hoped to have seen in this weird format, I saw," quarterbacks coach Dan Pitcher said, as the offseason program officially wrapped for the Bengals last week.

"There's that big void there of taking it to the field and doing it, but we have evidence of him doing it at arguably the highest level a college quarterback has ever done it six months ago. It is college football and the jump, but it's been what I expected, and he's pleasantly verified what I thought I was going to see."

'That interaction was so important'

When head coach Zac Taylor, Callahan and Pitcher huddled before this unprecedented offseason program, they set a goal to get as close to simulating the basics of an in-person offseason as possible for their new quarterback.

Some elements will just be impossible. There will be no learning from interceptions. There will be no showing off physical skills or limitations. There would be no football.

There would be four two-hour Zoom sessions per week.

But the advantage would be the program could focus on teaching the offense completely without interruption from practices, all the way down to explaining the library of drills that would be used whenever practice resumes.

"We got to have these lengthy conversations about a lot of things where you don't get the time to do that until they just come up and you are forced to do it," Callahan said of an installation that in an average year would be based around installing enough to be able to pull off the next day's practice. "He could wrap his brain around how everything that works for us and how he can manipulate it and spin for what he wants to do as a quarterback."

That includes talking through the creation of a playbook that brings to life concepts Burrow liked from LSU and meshing them into the Bengals' system.

"We looked at (LSU tape) with him and he was able to share his thoughts about what he really liked and wanted to continue doing," Pitcher said. "He and Brian would talk about it, say, 'We very easily can incorporate these because we already do something similar. Maybe these are new but worthwhile. These couple can go on the back burner.' It was a natural process that takes place."

Finding anything natural in this unnatural environment was considered a win. It's also why the staff came away excited by what they witnessed in Zoom walk-throughs that evolved over the last month.

Once they felt like Burrow was comfortable in the offense, they wanted to re-create what would happen on the field in a normal June.

Taylor and the staff mostly didn't want to come away from this program with teammates uncomfortable with Burrow's voice and communication skills, specifically his vocal relationship with center Trey Hopkins running the pre-snap routine.

So, they set up a Zoom call with the entire offense. With everyone looking at film of a play, they all would be muted except for Burrow and Hopkins. Taylor then would be on a FaceTime call with Burrow with his Zoom muted. The quarterback would have an earbud with Taylor's call acting as the helmet speaker.

Taylor would relay the call as the entire group looked at the play on film up on the screen. The play clock would start and then Burrow and Hopkins would need to work together to relay protections, audibles, checks and fire off the snap count.

A player at that point would be quickly asked to talk through their responsibility on the play or what they were thinking in the route or protection.

"It was interesting, for sure. You are trying to find every way possible to simulate him getting a play call in his ear and having to relay that information to the team and visual stimulus of a play in front of everybody," Pitcher said. "We had to be as inventive as we could be with some of that stuff ... I'm sure he had to let (his parents) know he was hollering out the cadence and not locked in a closet or something."

The staff can joke about the process, but the communication these exercises established has turned out to be quite valuable.

"That allowed Joe to call the play, he would be with the offense, they would hear him talk, they would hear his snap count," said Callahan, estimating they'd done this for some period of time every session since late May. "They'd hear all the things him and Trey would communicate about pre-snap. They would hear him talk through whatever the criteria was for any checks or audibles or whatever the protection calls were. Him and Trey would have a dialogue. Trey would start to point and Joe could trump it and change it and make it something else. Just to get that interaction was so important for a young quarterback, to be in front of the unit."

'I don't anticipate there being a lot of mental failing'

Taylor spent most of the spring bouncing around each positional meeting and probably spent more time listening to what was going on than in a normal year. There was no dropping in on each group without the interruption of the head coach opening a door or walking around halls.

With an increased involvement elsewhere, the coach left most of the schooling of Burrow to Pitcher and Callahan.

Outside of an early meeting when the first-year quarterbacks coach accidentally forgot to let Taylor into a QBs meeting for 15 minutes as the Zoom host, the results left everyone as confident as possible heading into the potential return of practice next month.

Rookie quarterbacks always go through the failing on the field while trying to gain instinctive knowledge of the system. The process has been inverted here, with the system fully going in first

and Burrow being able to take over on the field-work from this point forward.

This portion of the program played into his wheelhouse, but it will be interesting to see what kind of efficiency it creates in how fast he can start playing well between the lines.

"It's a unique case study," Pitcher said. "Something to this extent hasn't happened before. The failing — there's value in that. There's value in testing the physical limits. Seeing, OK, I'm going to fit this throw in there, not the best idea. Or maybe I can fit this throw in there. We are very fortunate working with Joe and his skill set, I don't anticipate there being a lot of mental failing when it comes to Joe. He works extremely hard — don't get me wrong, he's a rookie but he's going to make mistakes as any rookie in that are — but getting to work with him as much as we have between Zac and Cally and myself, I feel really good where we are at as far as that goes."

Many have wondered about Burrow getting the group of receivers together for a throwing session as we've seen other quarterbacks put together around the league — whether Josh Allen with the Bills in Florida or Matt Ryan with the Falcons in Atlanta.

The hope is a group, led by Burrow and A.J. Green, is aiming to throw something together after the Fourth of July holiday. Even just starting to establish chemistry and relationships will be a plus, but the logistics are still in motion and obvious uncertainties abound.

Regardless, when they arrive together whenever training camp or a potential earlier acclimation period begins, Burrow won't be coming in blind in the first steps toward establishing leadership and belief in his abilities from teammates and coaches.

He may be a rookie and treated like a rookie, but it's clear they are dealing with somebody different. The instinctual nature of Burrow's football knowledge, particularly in analyzing the big picture of every play, was the most obvious takeaway of the last few months.

"He's a coach's kid, so he's been hanging around football since he was a little kid," said Callahan, notably also a coach's kid, son of former head coach and current Browns offensive line coach Bill Callahan. "He's got such a feel for it. A lot of these things aren't new for him. Maybe the translation of how it hits his brain and word of it is different, but it's not new. He picks things up really quickly and has an analytical brain where once he has command of it, now he knows how to fit the pieces together. What if I do this and this in this situation? Great, I love that, that's what guys who have been playing for eight years do. The adjustments are so easy for him because he has such great understanding of how the pieces of an offense fit together versus a defense."

Callahan acknowledges Burrow probably got bored at times, not just from being tired of Zoom meetings along with the rest of the working world, but the coaches made a point to coach everyone at a rookie pace even though his thought process might be many steps ahead of those basics.

"Sometimes he would say things early on and I'd say, we are not talking about that right now, let's just get through what we need to get through here and then we can revisit that later," Callahan said. "We will probably answer that question you have in a day or two days or three days because we are not there yet. I know you are, but we're not."

There's only so much you can show in these sessions. The coaches used an app called Notability that allows you to share screens and write live with the Apple Pencil to simulate whiteboard work. They found that handy to help Burrow or Ryan Finley or Jake Dolegala work the board and constantly be teaching the plays and concepts back to the coaches.

Anything to break up the monotony.

The consistent takeaway from all the coaches involved was Burrow's unrelenting desire to make sure he had this system understood. That much was obvious. As was the advanced nature of his acumen.

These are all traits they knew they were getting from Burrow or had heard enough stories about during the draft process to assume it to be true, but to see it in motion in this unorthodox setting was striking.

"The ability to take a concept that takes some guys maybe an offseason to learn, it would take a huge concept and he's immediately thinking about the next level of things," Callahan said. "'What can I get to that's better than this? What if we get this coverage, I don't like this look here what can I do?' Well, here's your options. OK, good.

"His processing information and applying it to the next level was what was really impressive to me."

The field awaits. Putting the arm in lockstep with the brain comes next. He's still a rookie and nobody expects perfection. But he enters with a base of knowledge for what the Bengals are trying to accomplish that almost no rookie quarterback is afforded upon taking his first snap in a pro helmet.

Will that make a difference? Nobody knows. But forced by life to find a new way to groom a rookie quarterback, the Bengals did just that and feel as good as you can about what they were actually able to get from it.

Specifically, what Burrow was able to get from it. It lays the foundation of not just learning the offense, but also earning the respect of the entire team.

"He comes in right away because he understands all of it and he has a ton of confidence and a ton of command," Callahan said, "and I think those guys are immediately drawn to that." ▬▬▬

That's Our Boy!

Joe Burrow's Parents Determined to See Son Play in Person

By Jay Morrison

SEPTEMBER 22, 2020

Joe Burrow received his "Welcome to the NFL" moment on one of his first snaps in the Sept. 13 season opener when Chargers defensive tackle Jerry Tillery planted him for a 14-yard sack.

Burrow's parents, Jimmy and Robin, got their "Welcome to the NFL" moment a few days later in Cleveland.

Forced to watch their son's NFL debut on television because it was played without fans at Paul Brown Stadium, the Burrows were excited to make the drive from Athens, Ohio, to attend Thursday night's game against the Browns at FirstEnergyStadium.

"It was so nice to be able to be there, but it was a different kind of environment as far as the whole pro football fan situation," Robin said. "I hadn't really thought about whether it was going to be different from college or not, so that was interesting.

"It was a little bit harsh," she added. "That would be one way to put it. I guess I haven't been to enough NFL games to know if that's normal or if that's just a Browns thing. We experienced it a couple of times in college, but this was just different. That's OK, though. I'll have to thicken up my skin a little bit, I guess."

Sitting in Section 149 in the west end zone (the non-Dawg Pound end zone), Jimmy and Robin were sporting plenty of Bengals gear. But unlike their two seasons watching Joe play for LSU, at home at Tiger Stadium and at other SEC venues, they weren't wearing replicas of his jersey.

And that was by design.

"We're kind of waiting a little," Jimmy said. "We don't want to get too far out in front of ourselves, advertising that we're Joe Burrow's parents. Everybody at LSU knew it no matter what, so you might as well wear the No. 9. But that's not the case here."

They still got recognized quite a bit more than they expected even without the jerseys and with masks covering their faces, both in the seating area and out on the concourse going to the concession stands.

The people who knew who they were, or suspected it and asked, were friendly. Browns fans who just thought Jimmy and Robin were random Bengals supporters were the ones who got abusive.

But the Burrows said they were thrilled they got a chance to go and would do it again without hesitation.

"It was great to be there, it really was," Jimmy said. "After going to 15 games last year, it was tough missing the season opener. It just doesn't feel right sitting in front of the TV watching it."

The feeling was familiar in multiple ways for Jimmy. FirstEnergyStadium was where he took Joe to his first NFL game as part of a Christmas weekend doubleheader in 2006, a few weeks after his 10th birthday.

They watched LeBron James and the Cavaliers edge the Orlando Magic on Saturday night, then took in a Browns-Buccaneers game the following day on Christmas Eve to see Jimmy's good friend Gus Bradley, who was Tampa Bay's linebackers coach at the time.

Jimmy was responsible for Bradley getting his start in the NFL. The two had worked together at North Dakota State, with Bradley replacing Jimmy as defensive coordinator when Jimmy left for Ohio University in 2005.

Monte Kiffin was one of Jimmy's coaches at Nebraska and mentored him when he broke into coaching. Kiffin was looking for a quality control coach and had asked Jimmy about another coach, but Jimmy said the person he needed to call was Bradley.

"Monte asked him if he thought Gus could be his linebackers coach in a year or two, and I told him, 'He could be your linebackers coach right now,'" Jimmy said.

Jimmy took Joe to Cleveland again in 2011 to see Bradley, this time when he was in his third season as the defensive coordinator for the Seahawks. That was the game Joe pointed to when he was asked in a press conference leading up to his debut about the first NFL game he had attended. He forgot about the 2006 Cavs-Browns weekend.

The irony — or beauty, depending on how you want to look at it — of the 2020 NFL schedule is that Joe was going to get to make his NFL debut against Bradley, who is the Chargers' defensive coordinator. The Burrows had planned to make a weekend of it, meeting up with Bradley's wife, Michaela, who already would have been in Ohio that weekend to see the couple's son Carter, a sophomore quarterback at Toledo.

The Burrows would have been able to see Michaela and Carter on Saturday, watch Joe make his NFL debut on Sunday, then visit with Gus after the game. But the COVID-19 pandemic ruined all of it.

Not only were the Burrows not going to be able to watch Joe make his NFL debut in person, but they also had to scramble just to figure out how to watch him on TV. Their cable company in Athens broadcasts the CBS affiliate from Columbus, WBNS. With Fox having the Week 1 NFL doubleheader, WBNS had to choose between airing the Browns-Ravens game at 1 p.m. or the Bengals-Chargers at 4 p.m.

The station picked the Browns, forcing the Burrows to call an audible.

A few days before the game, they had DirecTV installed with the NFL Sunday Ticket. Asked if he had to drop any names or pull any strings to get the satellite installed so quickly, Jimmy laughed and said, "I'm not going to comment on that. Let's just say we got it done in time to watch."

And so after sitting in stadiums with almost 100,000 people and watching their son orchestrate the greatest season in college football history while leading LSU to the national title, Robin and Jimmy settled onto their couch to watch his debut on the biggest stage all alone. No family. No friends. Just them.

"We got invited to some people's houses and a couple people asked us to meet uptown to watch it, but the few times I watched him on TV, I just like to watch it by myself without a lot of distractions," Jimmy said. "So we just made the decision to experience the highs and lows just us two. It was exhausting, to be honest with you."

Jimmy had experienced it before. He was still coaching at OU during Joe's junior year at LSU and made it to only three of the 13 games.

But the Chargers game marked the first time Robin had not been there in person to watch Joe play, beginning from soccer in second grade on up through all the baseball, basketball and football games in middle school, high school and college.

There were a couple of Ohio State road games she didn't attend when Joe was redshirting and she knew he wouldn't play. But she was there every time he played.

And when Joe told them that Bengals players could get two tickets for the Week 2 road game at Cleveland, there was no way she was going to miss a second consecutive game, even if she had to pay for it a little bit Friday.

Jimmy is retired, but Robin still works as a school principal at Eastern Elementary School, about 30 miles east of Athens. And with the unusual blended learning schedule that the district and many others are adjusting to, Robin was committed to working full days on Thursday and Friday, even though her son had his first road, divisional and prime-time game in the NFL 3 1/2 hours away.

Jimmy picked her up when the school day ended Thursday, and they headed to Cleveland. After the game, they drove to a hotel in Canton, got a couple of hours of sleep, then headed south to make sure Robin was at school to greet the school buses at 7:15 a.m.

"It wasn't terrible until the middle of Friday afternoon," she laughed. "I really started losing my adrenaline. It was a long afternoon. But it was definitely worth the trip. I'll do it many times over if can watch him play."

Joe's first NFL touchdown pass came in the second quarter, and Robin got just as loud as she did when she sprang from the couch during his 23-yard touchdown run in the opener. The only thing that could have made being there in person for his first touchdown pass better would have been if it came in the end zone where they were sitting, not all the way at the other end of the field.

His two fourth-quarter touchdown passes came right in front of his parents in the west end zone.

"I don't even think he knew where we were sitting," Jimmy said. "We got the tickets emailed to our phones from the Bengals. He knew we were there somewhere."

So there was no wave or point or even eye contact after a big play.

Robin was OK with that, although she acknowledges that she thought about rectifying it given that seats were only about 50 feet from the tunnel where the Bengals ran on and off the field.

"I thought about walking down there, but I didn't want to embarrass him — 'Hey, Joe! Hey, Joe! It's mom!'" she joked. "It's just weird. Even through

college, I kind of felt like he was still just my little boy. But I don't feel that way anymore. I mean, he's still my son, obviously. But he's not my little boy anymore. He's out there with grown men. But it's still just as fun to be there, and we're going to go to as many of them as we can." ▬▬

Joe Burrow's Best

Bengals Coaches Detail Their Favorites From His First Half

By Paul Dehner Jr.

NOVEMBER 9, 2020

Joe Burrow's first half ranks as one of the best for a rookie quarterback in league history. Yards and touchdowns, highlights and hero ball, many reasons jump off the film to even the average viewer.

He consistently delivers the spectacular.

But what plays jumped off film to those working directly with Burrow since he was drafted first overall?

That was the question answered over the bye week as I asked Bengals head coach Zac Taylor, offensive coordinator Brian Callahan, assistant head coach/special-teams coordinator Darrin Simmons, quarterbacks coach Dan Pitcher and offensive assistant Brad Kragthorpe to pick and discuss their three favorite Burrow plays from the first half of the season.

"That's like choosing between your 10 kids who are your three favorites," Taylor said.

"Impossible to narrow down."

They did anyway.

"There's a million to choose from," Pitcher said.

Or at least tried.

"I kept it to six plays," Callahan said, "three mental and three physical."

Their deep dives and the variety of personal picks revealed that the intricacy and intelligence of Burrow's performance are where the true greatness lies.

Some are obvious. Other incredible plays come on a 2-yard gain on second-and-10. Or a quick pass to the flat on first down that was previously just a line in the box score. When details behind it emerge, suddenly, they come to life to showcase the beauty in Burrow's game.

The list resulted in a jersey-number-appropriate nine plays, all showcased for any combination of Burrow's athleticism and accuracy, confidence and chemistry, rebuttal and recall.

These were the most impressive plays of Joe Burrow's first half, through the eyes of those closest to him.

Play 1: 'This was a big moment for me watching his mental development'

- **Game:** Week 7 vs. Cleveland
- **Situation:** First quarter, 4:51, Bengals lead 7-0
- **Down and distance:** Second-and-10, Bengals 25-yard line
- **Result:** Complete pass in flat to Drew Sample for 10 yards.

Background: The previous week in Indianapolis, Burrow threw an interception against pressure that thwarted a potential game-winning drive, and in the film review he realized a specific check in his arsenal could have created an escape route, a quality play that could have avoided the worst, defining moment of the game. Fast-forward seven days.

Callahan: "Then it comes up a week later on second-and-10 in empty. We knew Cleveland was going to try to pressure us because they had some success the first time. You just have to show them you can handle it. We saw it during the week, any of these nickel pressures off the edge (No. 28), just check and get the ball out of your hand. We'll get 10 yards, 15 yards, easy. Just a long handoff. He diagnosed it, saw it, and those guys executed it. Threw right into the pressure, and we get 10 yards."

Background: The difference comes in the instantaneous reaction to seeing the nickel corner showing blitz. As soon as Kevin Johnson shows he is coming, Burrow fires off the check, the snap comes, and he throws it right over Johnson's head to Sample in the flat with blockers in front.

Callahan: "That's very discouraging for a defensive coordinator."

Background: This is quickly remembering a tool at his disposal that he could have used the previous week, going to it in the perfect situation, taking advantage of an overload pressure that had him exposed in the empty set. He beats it using his brain instead of his body.

Callahan: "These are the things that aren't noticeable on a global scale. Nobody is going to look at this play and say, 'Oh, shoot, what a play.' But people that know quarterbacking are going to look at it and say, 'Hmm, that's pretty damn good.' When you have a guy at the trigger that can process like this and see these things and do this type of stuff, it makes life so much easier on everybody. They get you out of bad plays and into good ones. This was a big moment for me watching his mental development of, 'I know how to take advantage of something. I've been presented a look. I know how to make it work for us.'"

Play 2: 'You only do this if you are so comfortable in your own backyard, playing with your friend that, I'm gonna try this'

- **Game:** Week 8 vs. Tennessee
- Situation: Fourth quarter, 9:06, Bengals lead 24-14
- **Down and distance:** Third-and-9, Titans 23
- **Result:** 17-yard completion to Boyd

Background: An obvious pick play. Maybe the best play of the first half for Burrow. Boyd is running across the field on a route that he catches a ton of passes on, but this is complementary to that and designed for him to put his foot in the ground and turn back the other way midway through. From there, the magic happens.

Taylor: "Joe knows that TB is being held. He knows where he is supposed to end up if he can get out of it. Joe pushes up, he lets the ball go at the moment he does, TB is not even close to coming out of his break. Joe just floats it as much as you can humanly float a football in a real, live game. This is like Backyard Football 101. You never really do this. You only do this if you are so comfortable in your own backyard, playing with your friend that, I'm gonna try this. That's really what he does. He puts so much touch on this thing and floats it to where if TB is ever going to be able to pull out and react, this is the only way it's going to happen. Sure enough, TB pulls out, it hits him right in the chest, he has no choice but to catch it."

Simmons: "If that ball is a foot further back to the right, the ball goes by Tyler and Tyler probably doesn't even know the ball is there. For him to put that ball in the spot he did with the touch he did in that situation is an unreal play to me. Unreal play. That's not something you can ever coach. That is just repetition and feel."

Taylor: "I just have such an appreciation for the confidence to throw that ball instead of just taking a sack like a lot of people probably would. Or waiting another second to see if he pulls away and therefore taking a sack. Or putting your eyes down and trying to find an escape route to get out of the pocket. It's just very rare that you would think, 'I'm going to give this guy a chance by throwing this touch and seeing if he can pull out of it.' It's borderline crazy."

Background: This also highlights another element that shows up frequently in coaches' comments as Burrow gets more reps with these receivers.

Taylor: "Another level to Burrow's game is how much he puts into receivers' body language and understanding how to read them, how they run their routes and get a feel for them and develop that chemistry. I do think it is different than a lot of people's approach. Not that every quarterback doesn't have that sense a little bit, but he does kind of deal with it on a different level with guys' body language or what they are doing that tells me when to throw this ball or where he is at. It's pretty impressive."

Play 3: 'It's such a unique example of mastering something'
- **Game:** Week 7 vs. Cleveland
- **Situation:** Fourth quarter, 4:23, Browns lead 31-27
- **Down and distance:** First-and-10, Bengals 37
- **Result:** 11-yard completion to Tyler Boyd.

Background: This might be the best example of savvy and recall all season, and it's a favorite of Callahan. Near the beginning of what ended up being a drive to tie the score in the final minutes, Burrow lines up with a two-man concept with Boyd and Mike Thomas on the left side.

It's one the Bengals actually ran in the first game against Cleveland in Week 2. That play came on fourth-and-4. Boyd took a pick play around toward the boundary, and Burrow hit him for a back-shoulder conversion.

On this play, Burrow checks over to the concept again since both Browns corners are pressing up against the receivers in man coverage, the same as they did in the first game. As soon as he does, Burrow notices the cornerbacks talking to each other in reaction to the signal. He feels like they also remembered what he was trying to do from the first game. He reads their reaction and immediately checks to a counter move off the play that allows Boyd to fake the boundary and cut back open over the middle.

Burrow was exactly right. The corner is caught sprinting toward the original play, and it leaves Boyd wide open coming back to the middle. This feels like an excellent time to remind everyone that this is the just seventh game of Burrow's NFL career.

Callahan: "You're constantly giving him tools in his toolbox he can get to whenever he wants. He sees press, checks it, realizes he checked to the same signal he did in the first game. Sees the communication and changes the play to the counter. It's such a unique example of mastering something. He's starting to master some of this stuff."

Background: Just the latest example of quick processing and recall, things that were among the biggest selling points on Burrow all the way back at the beginning of the draft process.

Simmons: "When we sat down and talked to this guy at the combine, you put plays up from this guy's season at LSU (and) you could show the original picture of the video that shows the scoreboard and down and distance. His recall, he can show you what the situation was, what the score was, what the flow of the game was and what they were trying to do and what happened. Not everybody can have that recall like that. That's why I think the guy's got a photographic memory of stuff he can pull from. It's really unique."

Play 4: 'There's just awareness of the pressure'
• **Game:** Week 2 at Cleveland
• **Situation:** Fourth quarter, 10:48, Browns lead 28-16
• **Down and distance:** First-and-10, Browns 31
• **Result:** 12-yard completion to Tee Higgins

Background: This one was a Taylor favorite, primarily for the insane number of boxes it checks in terms of playing the quarterback position and turning a potential negative play into a positive.

What most don't realize: What Burrow expected to happen at the beginning of this play did not occur, so he was immediately having to react on the fly against a nickel blitz that he knew was unprotected.

Taylor: "What I like about it, he puts two hands on the ball. Jonah (Williams) saves the day. He blocks Myles Garrett and blocks the nickel, which isn't necessarily his responsibility, he's just playing football. Joe is able to pull out of a really muddy pocket at that point, keep two hands on the ball, get his eyes down the field, get his shoulders turned, which is the hardest thing when you are throwing to your left as a quarterback when you are trying to move to your left and get the ball pushed down the field. It gets back (to Burrow resets to) throwing position, is able to get it to Tee for a 12-yard gain on a play that was supposed to go to the other side of the field versus a pressure we can't protect because we only have five blockers. And again, there's just awareness of the pressure. Ball security in the pocket, which is the No. 1 way fumbles occur, it's a quarterback in the pocket, but keeping two hands on the ball and being strong with it as you pull out, then keeping your vision down the field to identify some receivers and make sure we can get it completed and get a first down."

Play 5: 'He freaking ripped that thing'
• **Game:** Week 6 vs. Indianapolis
• **Situation:** First quarter, 0:50, Bengals lead 14-0
• **Down and distance:** Third-and-9, Bengals 31
• **Result:** 67-yard completion to Higgins

Background: The longest play of the season for the Bengals and the most obvious submission for this exercise. Yet the story behind the throw makes it all the better through the eyes of the coaches.

Taylor: "It appears to be a miscommunication on their end. ... Maybe they are throwing the coverage we anticipated, it's hard to tell, but the corner got a lot of depth there. Joe just threw it over the top, really, which was a little bit different than how we had worked it in practice. He had the confidence like, 'I'm throwing this ball if they give me any indication that it's there.' He had the confidence to rip it. Normally, a young quarterback would second-guess it. 'Hey, this isn't the exact look we talked about. I'm going to go to TB here or my checkdown and move on,' whereas Joe just said, 'I'm going to be aggressive if they give me any sort of a look. I'm throwing this ball to Tee.'"

Kragthorpe: "A lot of our go-balls had been back-shoulder, 50-50-type throws. As you saw on the tape, he threw that thing with confidence, too. Against a coverage that maybe that isn't where the ball 100 percent of the time should go, but he was confident in Tee and confident he was going to get in the corner. He freaking ripped that thing."

Pitcher: "I think if anybody who knows what they are looking at still had some reservations about the kid's arm strength, he should put to bed any reservations with that throw. It was a big-time throw to the field to a narrow window and a huge, explosive play."

Background: The Bengals were hammered the previous week by the Ravens' blitz packages and expected to see more. It was a disaster of a game in Baltimore, with the Bengals losing 27-3. They also had notably been awful throwing the ball 20-plus air yards to that point, hitting only one of 23 to start the year. This play, in particular, kickstarted the confidence that has fueled the offensive resurgence.

Pitcher: "The week before was kind of the one game that smacked us in the face a little bit and specifically smacked Joe in the face a little bit. His approach was great every week, but he came in with just a little bit more of exactly how you would expect a competitor like that to show up after getting our butts kicked."

Kragthorpe: "That was definitely one of those plays that gave us even more, was in that time we were starting to gain some momentum as an offense. That is one of those plays that made those guys feel like we are an explosive group."

———————— ————————

Play 6: 'It's almost like a sixth sense to him where he just feels things'
- **Game:** Week 8 vs. Titans
- **Situation:** Second quarter, 2:36, Bengals lead 10-7
- **Down and distance:** Fourth-and-5, Titans 43
- **Result:** 22-yard completion to Higgins

Background: A huge turning point in the Bengals' latest win. After this fourth-down conversion, they went on to score a touchdown with 32 seconds left and avoided the Titans matching before halftime, a portion of the game that has notoriously been a disaster area in Bengals losses.

As for the specific aspect of this play, the Titans used a three-man rush and Burrow ended up going an absurd six seconds from snap to throw.

Pitcher: "There's a fine line between looking at the rush and bringing your eyes down from what is happening down the field, which is not something that you want to do in most cases. But having an awareness of when you do have a three-man rush. When these guys are in these coverage areas, you intuitively realize, 'OK, there's only three rushing me.' You may never set your eyes on the rush itself, but you get that feeling. He understands that."

Callahan: "There's never panic. He feels a little push from the right side initially, and with this you can look at his growth a little bit, too. He feels the initial push a little bit, a natural rush ... so he moves off his spot. What he's done in previous games is he's stayed on the move. So he's run out to the numbers and allowed pursuit maybe to get to him. Now, all of a sudden, he stops and separates from where he felt the issue and sets himself back up. Now he's got all day because there's nothing over there. That to me is a little bit of his pocket growth. In college, these guys just run out there. And he's done that a couple times this year, probably to his detriment. Now he's slowed down, found himself a spot back and where the protection was and where he had the advantage and stayed there. I thought that was pretty cool on a developmental range."

Pitcher: "Next thing you know, the corner has had to cover for five seconds. It's an example of the guy just being a football player and knowing what to do in a lot of different situations."

Callahan: "He's got this kind of uncanny knack of knowing where everybody is and knowing where they are supposed to be. In this particular instance, Tee is on a fade route. He's not a part of this. He could have initially off the snap, but he's running out of there, we are trying to throw the ball to TB or Drew. When he moves and looks, now he sees, he checks his head twice, peeks to start, you see him glance at Drew and looks at the rush, he has both those guys over there. Then he stops and knows the only downfield option right now is Tee. He sees Tee start to break back in and just lets the ball go. And it's an unbelievable throw and catch. For him to know that Tee was downfield and at some point saw him break in, and then just to let the ball go as he feels it and throws a dime to Tee in between two defenders, it's almost like a sixth sense to him where he just feels things. He knows where everybody on the field is on both sides of the ball. He knows where they are, and then he feels guys move and separate. He doesn't have to see them."

Pitcher: "Just a big-time play in the game when you look back on it and really one he kind of made entirely himself. It's his ability to do that, not speaking for Zac, but as a play caller, if you know a guy has that in him, it gives you all the confidence in the world to be aggressive and know you don't have to have the perfect call every time and he's going to be smart and be aggressive when he can and make plays."

Callahan: "There are not many that do that the way he just did it right there."

Play 7: 'His understanding ... I think scares the hell out of opposing defensive coordinators'
• **Game:** Week 7 vs. Cleveland
• **Situation:** Fourth quarter, 2:15, Browns lead 31-27

• **Down and distance:** Third-and-11, Browns 24
• **Result:** 12-yard design draw for first down

Background: Bengals are driving for what ended up being the go-ahead touchdown pass to Giovani Bernard, but a false start put them in the long down and distance just outside the red zone. It's as big of a spot as you can be in. He sees the defense and moves to a quarterback draw (similar to how he ended up with his first career touchdown in the opener against the Chargers). The athleticism and guts it takes to eventually dive for the first down into two Browns coming at him speak for themselves.

What made it a favorite of the first half, however, was the background.

Kragthorpe: "That definitely sticks out more than any other in my mind. He got us into a quarterback draw. That was all him. That wasn't part of the play call. It was him just recognizing the defensive structure and getting us into what he saw was the best of a hittable play and converting a third down on a critical, critical moment. We are trying to go down and score and win the game, essentially. For him to do that, that was special."

Simmons: "His understanding of defenses at this point in his career and what defenses are trying to do, I think, scares the hell out of opposing defensive coordinators. Opposing defensive coordinators know and they feel it. They know it's just a matter of time before we can get all the pieces put together here (and) we are going to be something to be reckoned with. I've never been around someone that has the feel and understanding for offensive football this guy does."

Kragthorpe: "That would fall into his ownership of the offense and his comfortability. Being able to do those type of things. I'm not sure that is something he would have done the first or second week of the season. (Having) the confidence to do those types of things is something you see progress as the weeks have gone on."

---------- ----------

Play 8: 'It's subtle, but it makes all the difference in the world'

- **Game:** Week 6 at Indianapolis
- **Situation:** First quarter, 5:30, Bengals lead 7-0
- **Down and distance:** Third-and-7, Colts 34
- **Result:** 23-yard completion to Boyd

Background: The Bengals would go on to score a touchdown after this third-down conversion on the way to building a 21-point lead. Also, it's a perfect play to remind everyone that PFF has Burrow as one of the highest-graded passers in the intermediate range in the NFL. Plays like this are why.

Pitcher: "Thing that really stood out, we had really prepared him for a specific look on third down and given him some tools for how he could adjust the protection how he needed to see fit. So he saw a look, he made a change, and as is often the case, we talk about what we think is going to happen and there are times when we're right on the money, and those make you feel great as a coach. We gave you the answer to the test before it happened and it's easy. Go out there and make plays. Most of the time, it doesn't happen that way. There are shades of what you think are going to happen and other variables you didn't predict. This is one of those cases. Here's a tool you can use if you think you are getting a certain look, go ahead and use it, and then you can react if it doesn't happen. It didn't happen. But as he often does, he reacted on his feet and was able to use his eyes to move a linebacker and open up this giant void in the coverage to get us what turned out to be a pretty easy completion down the field to Tyler on that second drive."

Background: His immediate reaction holds the linebacker by looking in the flat, and then he drops the ball over the top of the linebacker in the middle of the zone.

Pitcher: "Evidence to me of, OK, this kid, not only is he prepared, not only is he ready to get to some of the answers we give him, but when it doesn't play out exactly like we think, he can think on his feet and make it happen anyway. Specifically, the eye manipulation that he used is something a normal Joe watching the game might not pick up on because it's subtle, but it makes all the difference in the world on a play over the middle of the field."

---------- ----------

Play 9: 'There are competitive guys and there are alphas. This guy is an alpha leader'

- **Game:** Week 8 vs. Tennessee
- **Situation:** Third quarter, 8:55, Bengals lead 17-7
- **Down and distance:** Third-and-10, Bengals 43
- **Result:** 8-yard run by Burrow

Background: OK, it would not be fair to ask all of Burrow's coaches about their favorite plays and not ask the quarterback himself. When I did, he went with a play that didn't even gain a first down. It was still pretty ridiculous to witness.

Burrow: "If I would've gotten a first down on that scramble last game, that would've been pretty cool. I would've liked that play, but I didn't get the first down. I don't know."

Background: Burrow said the moment when he knew he could play in this league came during that final drive of the opener that ended up an offensive pass interference call away from a winning touchdown pass.

Burrow: "I was struggling all game and then we put together a drive at the end and felt like we deserved to win that game (with) the way that we played on the last drive. But that really calmed my nerves and let me know that I could play at this level."

Background: Plays like the wild spinning off tacklers Burrow mentioned above, or the one he pulled off against the Eagles that would have turned into an explosive play had Higgins not stepped out of bounds, show off Burrow's athleticism. He concedes that is his most underrated trait, and his coaches agree.

Kragthorpe: "I 100 percent agree that's probably the most underrated aspect of his game is his athletic ability. All of those extended plays are stuff you can't coach. It's all him making plays when things aren't going to perfect."

Callahan: "He's a natural. Peyton (Manning), to me, is the best pocket mover I've been around. For as unathletic as he is as a pure athlete, his pocket movement was unbelievable. They just feel it. Joe has that natural feel. His eyes are downfield, he feels the rush and moves with some smoothness and he can get out of the pocket, he can run, he's not slow. He never timed his 40 at the combine because he didn't have to, but there are clips of him in that championship game, he outruns Isaiah Simmons to the sideline. His play speed is fast. His athleticism, lateral movement and quarterback movement skills are as good as anybody's."

Background: These types of plays and this type of confidence have created a genuine belief across the team that the Bengals are capable of playing

with anybody. It's a trait badly needed around these parts.

Callahan: "I think our guys are at the point now where they don't even think twice, we think whatever the down and distance is, he's going to find a way to get us out of it."

Simmons: "There are competitive guys, and there are alphas. This guy is an alpha leader. For a team to elect a rookie quarterback as a captain speaks volumes. The second he walked in the building. Always for rookie players, they are so worried they don't want to upset the balance of the team. I think this is a different situation. I think our team was looking for somebody to lead them. This guy has come in and done that. This guy walks in the building with that steely-eyed look on his face, and it never changes." ▬▬

The Blame Game

Joe Burrow's Season Ends Early After Substantial Left Knee Injury

By Paul Dehner Jr.

NOVEMBER 22, 2020

Everyone wants somebody to blame. He's the prince of Southeast Ohio and the player who's brought as much joy and hope to Bengals fans in this city as any player in 15 years.

On Sunday, fans watched Joe Burrow's left knee blown up in a gruesome twist of fate all too familiar to a franchise at times defined by quarterback injuries.

It hurts. Score another one for 2020. A roundhouse directly to the gut for everyone involved.

Somebody needs to be the target of the frustration, they say. Somebody needs to be blamed. Somebody needs to be fired for this feeling of emptiness thrust upon you.

I don't know what to say to people reading this story looking for that condemnation. Those decisions won't be made here or even in the coming weeks as the stages of grief transpire for the face of the franchise.

It needs to come from a place of logic and reality, one not many fans understandably deep in the bottle are feeling on a dark Sunday night.

The bottom line is if the second half of the season was about proof of concept for the coaching staff illustrating it can take Burrow and the franchise into 2021, that went off along with Burrow on the cart Sunday afternoon.

It makes the potential decision at the feet of the front office incredibly murky.

Are Zac Taylor and the coaching staff and the front office that plotted the course for the potential rookie of the year and No. 1 pick negligent in the injury that ended his season prematurely with a reported ACL tear? Did they take on too much risk in utilizing his incredible skill set?

Or is it football? Is it bad luck?

What the front office feels about that question will likely be the determining factor in how this year is judged and how the head coach is judged.

What we know is this: The Bengals trotted out an offensive line that wasn't good enough early in the season and gave up far too many hits on the quarterback while throwing it as much as any team in the game.

The line settled the past five weeks, as did the offense, despite a string of injuries and COVID-19 issues creating a rotation of different combinations. They ranked 15th in pass-blocking efficiency over the previous five weeks, according to Pro Football Focus.

They utilized a quick passing game as an extension of the running game and empty sets as a way for Burrow to counteract the lack of talent up front. It was working. In a three-game stretch against Indianapolis, Cleveland and Tennessee, the Bengals were second in the league in points per game. On Sunday against Washington, they moved every drive of the first half into position to score as Burrow threw 29 passes against 13 runs.

Burrow praised the play calling and his head coach in numerous news conferences after multiple games and many times during the week.

Still, it's Taylor's job to be the adult in the room, and if that strategy, with a substandard offensive line, jeopardized the health of the quarterback, it would be on his shoulders.

I asked Taylor if there was more he could have done to protect Burrow.

"All we can do is make progress as the season goes," Taylor said. "We gave up a lot of pressure in the beginning of the season. In these last couple weeks, our guys have done a great job of keeping people off Joe. He's had a great pocket. He did not have a sack in the first half. The hit, as I saw it, wasn't with the ball in his hand. People keep talking about the offensive line without seemingly watching the film for the last four weeks. Again, those guys have done a good job. It's been a revolving door of players. They have been doing a great job. Joe has done a great job moving us down the field. We felt like we were making a lot of progress over the last five weeks and we are not going to apologize for any of that."

Injuries stink. They are the worst part of football and particularly at quarterback, which serves as the engine for everything.

Was it Taylor's fault when Joe Mixon hurt his right foot for running him too much? Was it the coaching staff's fault when Sam Hubbard dislocated his left elbow for having him pass rush too much? When Carson Palmer tore the ACL in his left knee in the playoff game after the 2005 season, was that because of a poor offensive line?

No. They were doing what they do best and trying to help the team win a game. The same goes for Burrow. He was torching Washington's defense and wasn't sacked in the first half.

If Burrow throws 15 percent less this season, how much does that change the chances he still gets hurt? Minimal.

Taylor's job is on the line based on whether or not he wins games. There is zero doubt what was going on with Burrow was far and away their best shot to accomplish the task.

If fingers need to be pointed, you can direct them to a front office that spent large in free agency on the defense but settled for a backup in Xavier Su'a-Filo as their lone addition to the offensive line. They banked on unknown commodities to improve, like Michael Jordan, who has struggled to take the next step this season and was responsible for going to the ground, along with Washington's Jonathan Allen, directly into the left knee of the quarterback. The other side of the Burrow sandwich came from a sixth-round rookie, Hakeem Adeniji, getting beaten off the edge in his first start at right tackle after two quality showings on the left side. He was in at right tackle for — and later replaced by — Bobby Hart, a player with obvious limitations who was playing above expectations at times this year.

There was no serious attempt to find quality, trustworthy, upper-tier starters on the right side of the line to protect the franchise.

You'd assume there will be this offseason no matter what else is going on.

That said, I have a hard time thinking the front office could blame the coach for using the pieces it gave him and an offense that was as dynamic as any around here since 2015 the past five weeks.

Only director of player personnel Duke Tobin and the Brown family know what they are feeling right now, and their feelings are the only ones that matter in regards to the direction of the franchise.

After Sunday, the rest is suddenly unknown and massively frustrating for an organization that felt it was about to turn the rebuilding corner.

That's the worst part of this. Now we can only wonder if they actually were.

There's no judging anyone or anything by what's about to happen in the next six weeks. Nobody cares about a team rallying around Ryan Finley or whatever that's going to look like and Bengals fans for the most part won't be paying attention anyway, that's for certain.

So, what happens next? Nobody knows, but there is a certain point where 4-21-1 is ugly to overcome in any circumstance.

Fans are mad. Everyone is frustrated and feels snakebitten by a gross turn of events.

Sports stink like that sometimes, more often than fans around here would like. The Bengals need to do better in protecting Burrow. We knew that already. They are currently in line to have the third pick to make it happen.

You can better judge who is most to blame for this ending over the course of time when emotion subsides. And the answer could be the staff, the front office, the Curse of Bo Jackson or nobody at all.

For now, the pitchforks are out and the worry the Bengals could botch the gift of Burrow hangs over the day and however many months until the quarterback emerges fully healed.

There's precedent to believe, as he tweeted, he will be back next year, and the Bengals will be set up for his second-season spike with much more talent than surrounded him this year. An ACL tear is not a death sentence in the least.

Sometimes injuries happen. Is that the case this time? An injury happened? Everyone has an opinion on that. The only opinion on that question that matters resides in the offices of Paul Brown Stadium with a river view. ▬▬

THE PATH TO THE SUPER BOWL

'He Has an Aura About Him'

Joe Burrow Recruits as Bengals Build Team in His Image

By Paul Dehner Jr.

MARCH 20, 2021

Inside Jeff Ruby's The Precinct Steakhouse on Thursday evening, the Cincinnati Bengals' recruitment press dominated the room. Multiple tables, coaches, wives, four free agents who signed earlier in the day and prospective right tackle Riley Reiff, still contemplating if this is the city where he wants to spend his 10th NFL season.

In a week laced with unfulfilled hopes in reconstructing the offensive line and a market definitely dropping off beyond the former Minnesota Vikings tackle, the tension of landing Reiff loomed larger than his 6-foot-6, 305-pound frame.

The Bengals staff needed to show everyone in the room, specifically Reiff, what they all believe in. They needed the best recruiting tool in their arsenal.

Cue Joe Burrow.

"He has an aura about him," free-agent cornerback Mike Hilton said. "He's a young guy, but he commands the room."

He commanded these tables inside The Precinct dining room just as he did the locker room and field last year for the Bengals. Those closest to Burrow feel connected to a humility and presence that makes believers of everyone.

He did it at LSU. He did it in Cincinnati. On Thursday, he did it with Reiff.

"Went out to eat with him last night, had a good steak, I went away from eating that steak and I was like, 'I want to block for this guy,'" Reiff said Friday, minutes after signing his contract. "Seeing him on the film, but he's even better off the field."

Commanding a room is made easier, I suppose, when people are ordering a steak named after you. And it's delicious.

"Jeff Ruby's is the most fire steakhouse I've ever been to, I had the Steak Burrow," cornerback Chidobe Awuzie said. "I have never had a steak like that."

Thursday and Friday culminated a critical week in the moving of the Bengals roster under head coach Zac Taylor from the farm to the table.

The full, methodical turn out of the Marvin Lewis era was made complete this week.

A.J. Green signed in Arizona. Geno Atkins was released. William Jackson III went to Washington, Carl Lawson to New York. Only three players remain under contract from the team's last playoff appearance in 2015 (Giovani Bernard, Clark Harris and Trey Hopkins). Only 13 players remain who played a down for Lewis.

When players would walk into the locker room the past two years, reverence and respect would instantly be given to Green and Atkins. They deserved it. They were legendary here. Faces of the organization and potential future Hall of Famers. Any desire to take hold of the direction of the team and assert yourself as a leader would come with hesitancy as their veteran presence dominated the building.

With those names and memories of a bygone era out the door, there is only one face owning the direction of the franchise. While the Burrow started his era and built a presence last year as a rookie captain, in some ways, he was officially knighted Thursday at The Precinct.

"He played well this season. Guys around the league took notice of it," offensive coordinator Brian Callahan said of Burrow's presence commanding the room of free agents Thursday. "Obviously, his reputation preceded him from what he did at LSU. The whole world was watching that.

So he's got a reputation, and guys respect the way he plays the game. And then on top of that, he carries himself like a starting quarterback in the NFL that's going to do a bunch of great things in his career would carry himself. So everybody feels that, and they see that. It's fun to see guys react to him that way. It's the way I've always felt about him from the minute I met him. I think that's probably going to be a common theme as guys get to know him more and more and he continues to play better and better."

It worked with Reiff and his four new teammates.

"The kid's a killer," said Larry Ogunjobi, who chased Burrow around twice this past year with the Browns. "He's the real deal."

Awuzie said he sees something special brewing in Cincinnati, and that was a major part of the draw. As for why ...

"First off, let's start with the quarterback and what he can do," Awuzie said.

"Checks his ego at the door," new defensive end Trey Hendrickson said.

The attitude particularly attracted Reiff. A man from Parkston, S.D., and a product of the University of Iowa who has played his entire professional career in Detroit and Minnesota connected instantly with the guy from southeastern Ohio.

"Just the way he conducts himself, carries himself," Reiff said. "Seems like a down-to-earth, Cincinnati-type guy."

Those words jump off the page. A Cincinnati-type guy. Yes, the city and this team under Taylor are developing a type of player in the image of their quarterback. But what exactly is a Cincinnati-type guy?

"Tough, Midwestern, blue-collar. Comes to work," Reiff said.

Man, put that on a wall somewhere. Scrub "Seize The Dey" and replace it tomorrow.

The more Burrow recruits, the more Burrow wins, the more the Bengals believe they can build a team in his image. One that inevitably follows his example as the star in the room.

"I can just tell how genuine of a guy he is and how much he loves football," Hilton said, "so when you got a leader like that, you know he's leading the right direction."

Last year in free agency, the Bengals sold the hope and potential of Burrow. This year, they sold the guy. The proof. The personality. The owner of the room.

In a week when the Bengals cleared the runway for Burrow to take over as the face — and lead recruiter — for the organization, they can only say so far, so good.

"He certainly has tremendous impact when you got a quarterback that you believe in," Taylor said. "Everybody in the organization, everybody in the city believes in the guy. He believes in himself, and so that is very clear to those that are considering the Bengals and want to be a part of this. He's certainly a great draw because we know with him we can do a lot of special things here." ▬▬

Bouncing Back

How the Bengals Put Joe Burrow Back on the Field So Quickly

By Paul Dehner Jr.

AUGUST 10, 2021

When the Bengals' team conditioning test arrived on July 24, director of rehab Nick Cosgray went through his normal routine for the beginning of training camp.

But, for him and the Bengals training staff, this wasn't just another day.

They passed a milestone with Joe Burrow fully cleared for the open of camp, arguably the most high-profile, scrutinized rehab in their decades-long tenure at the club. They saw Trey Hopkins pass the test, fully cleared, just seven months since the starting center tore his ACL in the second half of the final game of the season.

Days later, when the first camp practice officially took place, Burrow and Hopkins both touched the ball on the first snap.

By the time the drenched towels of conditioning-test sweat returned to laundry bins inside the stadium, safeties coach Robert Livingston called Cosgray.

"He said, 'Nick, today was your Super Bowl,'" Cosgray said, who also saw 325-pound defensive tackle D.J. Reader pass the test coming off a quad injury. "And you know what, yeah, it kind of is. When those guys are able to get back out there and you see them and you see them succeed and do well it is kind of like the Super Bowl."

The vast majority of Bengals fans don't know Cosgray, head trainer Paul Sparling and assistants Dan Willen, Roberto Cardona and Michael Houk or strength and conditioning coach Joey Boese. They blend as anonymous blurry faces behind the portrait mode of your favorite players.

For some players, however, they are the most important faces at Paul Brown Stadium.

Hopkins, the 6-foot-3, 316-pound center stood in front of reporters with a smile stretching ear to ear on that first day of camp. The second sentence out of his mouth mentioned Cosgray.

"Especially Nick," Hopkins began. "Me and Nick everyday just really grinding and having that goal in mind that I want to be back. Nick let me know it's going to be tough, I'm going to push you when necessary, we got to be smart about things, we got to be smart about everything. And guys, I feel great. I can't say thank you enough to Nick and all the guys."

Those words are meaningful, not just as a polite recognition of those who helped through a rough time, but another trophy in the mantle of building trust between player and rehab staff that is essential to the entire operation.

Hopkins had the surgery done by Bengals team doctor Marc Galloway, stayed in Cincinnati and did all his rehab with Cosgray and the team trainers.

Players don't always stay in-house. Many agents have preferred doctors, and everyone knows the list of experts for certain ailments. When a player returns from an ACL tear in this short amount of time under the direction of the team, everyone wins. Hopkins' rehab becomes teach tape for overcoming injury.

A perfect recipe like this one with Hopkins is cooked with one primary ingredient.

"Attaining the trust of the athlete: That's critical," Sparling said. "If you don't have the trust of the athlete you are better off sending them someplace else, to be quite honest. It takes time to develop that trust."

Time didn't exist with their star quarterback.

The face of the franchise had his surgery done in December in Los Angeles and could have basked even longer in the Southern California sun while going through the formative stages of the rehab. Instead, the Ohio kid beckoned back to Cincinnati.

Suddenly, a player who almost never went through the training room during his rookie year was plopped into the lap of this staff with the eyes of every person in the organization — and around the NFL — upon them.

Sure, Burrow worked in conjunction with Dr. Neal ElAttrache, the surgeon to the sports stars in L.A., but this was now in the hands of Cosgray and the Bengals staff.

None of the basics changed in how they handled his ACL rehab compared to all the others that have come through over the years. Sparling, now in his 43rd season, has been a part of nearly every one.

But make no mistake, this one was different.

"Well, if anybody said there wasn't pressure they'd be frickin' lying," Sparling said. "You got a lot of people counting on you."

Every detail and decision earns extra scrutiny and conversation. There were extra conversations necessary that didn't come up with someone like Hopkins or C.J. Uzomah rehabbing his Achilles.

"Some of the requests that come along when you are dealing with a guy: 'Can we film this part of his rehab? Can we do this? People are interested, people want to know.' Sometimes for guys like us, myself, Joe, we don't care," Cosgray said. "I don't care that the people want to know how Joe is doing. I understand that side of it but to me, Joe and I know how he is doing and he's making progress and I don't care that everybody needs to know how he is doing."

Even one slow-motion Twitter video of Burrow walking into the building earned the thoughts of Internet MD. The eyes and ears of opinion and perception do add to the stress of going through this with a player of Burrow's status. As much as the Bengals tried to keep things insular, it's tough to do.

Case in point: even as Burrow blew expectations away going through the offseason rehab and spring practices, he's been forced to rehab the mental side of getting used to the pocket and being around a pass rush with his knee all over again in front of everyone in camp, as Burrow described himself Saturday. It's not always been pretty and often frustrating — words that can be said about the beginning of nearly every stage of rehab.

"Somebody just came in and said one of our players did an interview today and said something about Joe, 'Holy crap, it's all over that he's not comfortable,'" Cosgray said. "C'mon, who's not comfortable coming back from nine months and an injury like he had? Nobody is comfortable yet. It's a process. You get comfortable by doing it ... What are we looking at now that's saying he's not still exceeding expectations? The guy is back out there on the field after a really significant injury at prior to nine months, he's running around, he's cutting, he's throwing deep balls, shorts balls. He's an NFL quarterback at less than nine months after a significant injury. Everybody probably wants him to be completing every single pass, but I think he is where needs to be at this stage in the game. We have how many weeks before the season starts? To me, I watch him out there and I think he is doing extremely well."

— A —

Cosgray admits he sees these players differently than most. Not only does he view it through the context of hundreds of rehabs during his time with the Bengals, but as someone with a full understanding of the mental and physical evolution of each process.

"That's obviously someone that doesn't get enough credit for what he's done for this organization throughout the years," Giovani Bernard said last year. Bernard tore his ACL on Nov. 21, 2016, (Burrow was Nov. 22) and returned for the beginning of camp, building a bond with Cosgray in the process. "He's obviously a guy I trust a lot in what he tells me to do."

There's that word again: trust.

"The players have a lot of faith in him," said coach Zac Taylor, who admits he also puts a ton of faith in Cosgray as the connection to the process for him over the offseason, as he doesn't want to bombard the player with constant questions about the knee. "You can tell those guys that go through the process that come out, maybe they didn't know him as well coming into it, and then when they end the process, they are like, 'Man, he's a rock star.'"

Sparling insists they have an incredible staff and they can drive success stories like this one, but the trainers don't deserve the credit for these quick returns. They merely set the guardrails. The player must do the work. Part of what made the difference for Hopkins and Burrow was powering through the toughest times trusting the direction and people who set the parameters.

That includes knowing when to keep it light. Knowing when to push. Knowing when to tell the player to get away from the stadium for a week. All of those elements were part of these rehabs. For Hopkins, feeding off the progress of Burrow made a difference.

"Joe was a little bit farther ahead than I was," Hopkins said, "but it was good to look into the future those couple of weeks and be like, 'OK, this is where I should be at. This is what he's doing. This is what I should be able to do in a couple of weeks.'"

Burrow's focus left an impression on everyone that came in contact with him. So, when it was posed to Burrow at the start of camp if he was grateful to be back, that didn't quite connect.

"I don't know if grateful is the right word," he said. "A lot of hard work went into that. Grateful to me seems like there was a lot out of my control. And I worked really hard to get here. I had great people around me that worked really hard to get here. There's a lot of hard work from a lot of different people that helped me. So I am grateful for the help that I had. But I also put in the work."

A fact those closest to his rehab knew all too well.

"Joe was a pro, my God, he makes it so damn easy," Sparling said. "I told him, 'You are going to make us all look good.' Trey is the same way. When you are working with pros like that, it takes out some of the uncertainty and challenges. We didn't have to deal with challenges with either one of those guys once they got here because they just went after it."

Once Burrow, Hopkins, Reader — and a few days later injured defensive tackle Renell Wren — passed their physicals, a new collection of players and relationships cycled to Cosgray and the rehab staff. Larry Ogunjobi showed up with a hamstring and returned on Monday. Cam Sample worked through his. In camp, Cosgray is in at 5 a.m. every day, knowing he won't be leaving until after 9 p.m.

Every day is long and filled with new relationships to build and trust to develop.

That's part of why July 24 was the Super Bowl. The entire team saw Burrow on the turf in Washington last season. They saw Hopkins take on what the center called the "gut-punch" and "short straw" in the final minutes of the regular season. What happened with their remarkable returns speaks louder than words any player can say. Even though the players can still say plenty.

"I got a lot closer with Nick," Hopkins said. "This wasn't even my first injury working with him. Nick rehabbed me through my tibia fracture my rookie year. But just being here, being older I think and being a rookie and being hurt really sucks because you don't even know where you're at. Being a little bit older and being able to talk about things and life experiences, and learn about him, where's he's at with him and his family. That was a really cool experience."

Not all long rehabs develop into friendships. Some players don't feel the need to be extroverted during those long months of working back. But, in this case for Hopkins and Burrow, it helped.

"He's hilarious, very sarcastic, which is my kind of person. I love sarcasm," Hopkins said of Burrow, then turning to the tone of every day at the stadium. "I love the jokes. It just makes the day better. When you laugh with somebody while you're working, while you're going through the dog days ... you don't really feel good. Your knee is achy. It's tight but you can crack jokes. Laughter makes everything a little bit better, makes it a little bit easier."

Not that Cosgray, Sparling or anyone on the training staff is looking for anybody to sing praises about their experiences. They signed up to be the guy behind the guy. Fitting then, watching in the background creates some of the proudest moments of their year.

"We work in a thankless business, right?" Cosgray said. "People expect you to do your job. Guy is supposed to rehab, they are supposed to be back on the field and people expect that to happen. But it is pretty cool for me and for I think our entire staff, you put so much time and effort and you get to know these guys on a very personal level. You become friends with them. You want to see your friends do well."

In rehab and friendships, the worrying and monitoring never ends. Even after the Super Bowl.

Especially when one of those friends wears No. 9.

"They do everything you ask them to do and they are doing it well and then it's like we worked hard and did everything the right way, but you still are kind of holding your breath a little bit," Cosgray said. "Obviously, I have the utmost confidence that everybody we put back on the field is ready to go. They wouldn't be back out there if you weren't, but you are still sitting here with your fingers crossed a little bit just saying, 'Hey, everybody stay away from him.'" ▬▬

Altering the Equation

Joe Burrow Returns in Dramatic and Memorable Fashion

By Paul Dehner Jr.

SEPTEMBER 12, 2021

Joe Burrow walked into the postgame news conference room and listened as Ja'Marr Chase finished his session with the media.

After Chase was done, the two walked past each other, gave their pinky celebration they've been doing since their LSU days and the quarterback sat down.

"I thought he was dropping everything," Burrow said with a wry smile.

The only thing missing was a sip from the bottle of water or puff from a cigar to recreate one of his most famous memes from LSU.

He oozed understated swag slouched in the chair only moments after one of the ballsiest throws by a quarterback in the recent history of Paul Brown Stadium, checking to a 26-yard toss on fourth-and-an-eyelash with the game hanging in the balance.

C.J. Uzomah casually referred to Burrow as "Franchise" while sitting in that same chair after the Bengals' 27-24 overtime win against Minnesota.

Indeed. Returning nine months after a gruesome torn ACL and MCL, with a team admittedly motivated by his every word, Burrow took five sacks and two more hits from a Mike Zimmer defense sending free runners at his repaired left knee.

Burrow even took a hit that rolled up his ankle, and he had to limp toward the sideline while holding his shoulder but just hopped on the stationary bike behind the bench and kept pedaling.

"My adrenaline kicked in," Burrow said. "We were good to go after that."

A city prepared to gasp every time Burrow took a hit only saw his toughness topped by his bravado.

He eventually stood in for the best passer rating (128.8), completion percentage (75) and yards per attempt (9.7) of his career, connected with Chase on the deep ball months in the making that sent Bengals fans into hysteria and put the game on his back in the most important moment of the day.

"When the game is on the line," Burrow said, "I like the ball in my hands."

Everyone does. Burrow reminded the league on Sunday how much different this franchise looks and feels in his hands.

"We trust Joe with everything that we're about," head coach Zac Taylor said.

This game was supposed to be about judging how Burrow looked and felt adjusting to the mental side of playing on the knee again. Or how long it would take him to get on the same page with Chase coming off the No. 5 pick's headline-driving, sluggish preseason. Yet, here was Burrow spinning away from free blitzers for 12-yard completions, throwing a 50-yard touchdown dime to Chase and gritting through injury to pull off a win he knew this team had to have.

"I don't think he feels any standard or pressure from the outside world," said Joe Mixon, who ran 29 times for 127 yards at 4.4 yards per carry. "I feel like he put a lot of pressure on himself, and even in the fourth quarter or overtime, I was telling him, 'Bro, come on, you got to lead us. It's that time. This is what you are made for, this is who you are, this is what you do you. You come here and make plays.' And he led us."

He led them to 27 points against one of the best defenses they will face all season.

This goes beyond throws or audibles or even the remarkable recovery to reach this point. It's the way he pulled everyone along with him.

Burrow dropped the line about Chase as a subtle I-told-you-so at all the noise circulating, but he stood stoutly in his corner through every drop and problem that unfolded through camp. He worked with him after practices and kept his head up during the preseason games. He stayed there with even more confidence Sunday.

"I had a couple guys come up to me and say, 'I hope Ja'Marr comes to play today,'" Burrow said. "And I said, 'Don't worry. It's Sunday. It's game day. He's going to come here to play.'"

Burrow hit one touchdown pass longer than 20 yards in the air all of last season then worked all offseason even during his grueling rehab to improve in that area. The deep ball to Chase now equals last year's total. It made that one play extra special.

"Yeah, it really was," Burrow said. "Ja'Marr caught me on the sideline and said he was glad I didn't overthrow him. And I said, 'Come on, man. How many times have we done this? We've done it over and over again.'"

Burrow also used his cadence as a weapon to draw the Vikings offside to pull off the other longest gain of the day, but it won't show up in the books. After getting the Vikings to jump, he used the free play to throw a jump ball to Tee Higgins that drew a pass-interference penalty on Bashaud Breeland and essentially created the eventual 2-yard touchdown pass to Higgins for their first score of the game.

More hidden yards, more hidden impact.

During the week, he forced the offense to run through what ended up being the game-winning play an extra time against air because he didn't like the way it looked one time when he saw it in practice. That ended up paying off in the most important moment.

Those details in the shadows showed up in the spotlight.

The Bengals looked relevant Sunday. They played with excitement, energy and tenacity that makes you believe they might replicate it many times over. Thanks to the instant answering of questions by "Franchise" on Sunday, there's a reason to believe they do. A fact not lost on No. 9.

"Remember earlier in the week when you guys asked me how important winning the first game was, and I shorted you out? Well, the first game's really important," Burrow said with a laugh. "You need momentum early in the season to gain more and more momentum — it keeps snowballing. We felt giving up a big lead, coming back and winning the game and making big plays when they count, it's going to serve us well going forward."

Forward feels like a different concept with Burrow brashly at the forefront, again his authentic, confident, unapologetic self and injury in the rearview mirror. We may have known this before, but Sunday's roars in Cincinnati served as a powerful reminder.

"We've got Joe Burrow at quarterback," Chase said. "That's a real quarterback. We've got nothing to do but lean on Joe and have Joe tell us what to do." ▬▬

The Big Payback

Joe Burrow Makes and Erases History at the Same Time in Bengals' Beatdown of Ravens

By Jay Morrison

OCTOBER 24, 2021

When Joe Burrow tore his ACL 11 months ago, there were a lot of negative thoughts filtering through his brain.

There was the dread of a long and grueling rehab. The fear that came with the uncertainty of whether he would ever be the same. And right there at the top of the list, the stinging regret of not getting a second chance to prove himself against the team that not only made him look lost and confused but delivered one of the most severe beatings he's ever absorbed on a football field.

Burrow made his return Sunday afternoon to Baltimore, the scene of last year's Week 5 crime where the Ravens sacked him seven times and hit him an additional eight while coloring his jersey green with M&T Bank Stadium turf.

Burrow returned for payback. And he got it. And then some. He wasn't just better, he was as good as he's ever been on an NFL field. He roasted the Baltimore defense for a career-high 416 yards and three touchdowns in a 41-17 victory that not only put the Ravens on notice that there's a new contender in the AFC North, it let the rest of the NFL know that the idea February football for Cincinnati has legitimacy.

"Obviously last year wasn't very fun," Burrow said. "Today was a lot of fun."

"When I got injured last year, that was one of the things I was most upset about was not getting a chance against our division multiple times," Burrow added. "I've always felt like the more I play, if you give me two chances against a team, I'm going to play much better the second time. That's just common sense in my head, and I didn't get that chance against Pittsburgh and Baltimore last year."

The game he played against the Steelers last year wasn't much fun either. It was seven days before the Washington game where he shredded his knee, and the Steelers sacked him four times and registered nine quarterback hits as Burrow went 21 of 40 for 213 yards and a 76.4 rating, the third-lowest of his rookie season.

When he got his second crack at the Steelers in Week 3 this year, Burrow was 14 for 18 with three touchdowns and a 122.9 rating, the second-highest of his career at the time.

What he did Sunday against the Ravens was similar in scope yet paled in comparison as he not only set a career high with 416 yards, he became just the eighth quarterback to ever throw for that many yards against a Baltimore defense. He was also the only opponent in the Ravens' 26-season history to throw for more than 400 yards with three touchdowns.

This wasn't just redemption. It was domination.

Although it started off looking like repetition. The Ravens came after Burrow early and hit him often on an eight-play series to open the game.

"The first drive, he got hit, and there were some communications issues we had to iron out," Bengals head coach Zac Taylor said. "Their complex blitz packages, they're very good at it. They get free runners coming in on quarterbacks for years. But our guys, we felt did a good job of coming to the sideline and communicating, fixing that, and keeping some tough hits off Joe."

And when Burrow is free to assess, adjust and accelerate, special things happen.

The Bengals hadn't scored a touchdown in 33 consecutive drives against the Ravens, a streak of futility that predated Burrow. But when he hit tight end C.J. Uzomah for a 55-yard touchdown with 6:29 left in the first half, it started a stretch of five touchdowns on seven possessions.

Burrow never even had a stretch of five completions in seven attempts in his first game against Baltimore. To go from that to five touchdowns in seven drives against that defense is unbelievable.

Unless you're Ja'Marr Chase.

"I expect Joe to be like this," said the rookie wide receiver who accounted for nearly half of Burrow's passing yards with a career-high 201 on a career-high eight catches.

"I expect nothing less," Chase continued. "I expect him to come out of every game with his A-game, as he would expect of me."

Just as Chase helped Burrow break all kinds of records at LSU, Burrow is driving Chase deeper and deeper into history every single week. No receiver has had more yards in the first seven games of his career than Chase's 754. And it's not even close. Anquan Boldin had the previous Super Bowl-era record of 621. The previous all-time NFL record belonged to Harlon Hill (685 in 1954).

Only Martavis Bryant had more touchdown catches (seven) through his first seven games than Chase's six. And Chase's 82-yard touchdown reception against the Ravens was his eighth catch of at least 30 yards, one more than Randy Moss and Stefon Diggs had in the first seven games of their career.

It's all been fueling the hype and hyperbole machine, with Burrow drawing comparisons to Joe Montana and Chase to Jerry Rice.

"Let's relax with all that," Burrow said when the comparisons weren't mentioned again after the win. "Let me be me."

As easy as it is to be awed by the numbers the duo is once again putting up after doing the same thing at LSU, what they did Sunday was only half of the story. On a day when Chase became just the ninth player in Bengals history to record at least 200 receiving yards in a game, Burrow still managed to spread the ball around in impressive fashion, picking apart the Baltimore defense as much as plunging in for the deep cuts.

On the field goal drive right before halftime that answered the Ravens' first touchdown and gave the Bengals a 13-10 lead at the break, Burrow's six completions went to four different receivers.

"I don't know what the statistics are with this, but at the end of the half, we have to be up there with putting points on the board," Uzomah said, correctly.

The Bengals are tied with the Saints and Packers for second in the league with 34 points scored in the final two minutes of the first half. The Browns are first with 42.

"That's something we pride ourselves in," Uzomah added. "We know that's stealing a possession, really, by going down, executing a two-minute drive, and putting points on the board. That's huge going into the half. We view that as a victory for us whether it's seven or three."

In previous weeks, it's been the deep-ball explosions to Chase. Sunday was a tougher slog, which just accentuates Burrow's evolution.

The Bengals also scored on their first drive of the second half, and in a much quicker fashion, needing just three plays. It was another data point in what makes Burrow so lethal when he gets a second look at something.

Seeing the Ravens preparing to crash a wide receiver screen, Burrow audibled to pass to Uzomah up the screen. Uzomah ran right past charging safety Chuck Clark, and Burrow hit him for a 32-yard touchdown.

Burrow confirmed the audible in his postgame press conference. Asked if the original play was the wide receiver screen the Ravens thought they had sniffed out, Burrow just smirked and said, "Yeah, something like that."

It brought back strong vibes from the smug smirk as Burrow sipped from a water bottle at LSU.

Sunday's game looked a lot like that run to the Heisman and national championship. This wasn't a bad Lions defense or undermanned Jaguars unit. This was the Ravens, and they didn't stand a chance against a hellbent-on-redemption Burrow.

One of the constants with Burrow through the years is the bigger the stage and the brighter the lights, the better he plays. And until he gets a chance to do it in the postseason, playing a division opponent on the road with first place in the division on the line is as big as the stage gets.

He's now faced each division opponent twice. Cleveland was the only team he got to play both games against last year.

His completion percentage (60.7 to 74.5), passer rating (90.6 to 112.5), yards (316 to 406) and yards per attempt (5.2 to 8.6) also rose dramatically.

"You saw against the Browns last year I got better from Game 1 to Game 2, and that's what I'll try to do going forward," Burrow said.

Mission accomplished Sunday in Baltimore. And then some.

"We had a great plan," Burrow said. "Coaches did a great job with putting together a plan that I felt good about, and we felt good about, and we knew what (the Ravens) do is they make you, they put you in a lot of one-on-one matchups, so you have to win, and that's why guys get paid. You've got to go win the one-on-one matchup, and we have guys that did that today in the second quarter and the second half. We really won all of our one-on-one matchups that really mattered. (Baltimore) puts the most pressure on you of any team that I've played in the league, and we really responded today."

Of all the things Burrow does well, responding is near the top of the list.

He did it against Pittsburgh in Week 3, and Sunday in Baltimore.

"It feels very similar," Burrow said. "We played a lot better on offense today than we did against Pittsburgh, but now our defense has proven to be one of the top ones in the league, and it feels good to go 2-0 against those guys.

"But the great thing about the NFL, we've got to play those guys again later in the year, so we know that they're going to be ready as well as Pittsburgh, so really we've got to just keep getting better."

At some point, it might be fair to question if that's even possible.

For now, however, Bengals fans should be thrilled with the fact that it's merely probable. ▰▰▰

Contenders

With Joe Burrow, the Bengals Can Make a Super Bowl Run

By Paul Dehner Jr.

JANUARY 2, 2022

Zac Taylor sat down at the podium in the Bengals press room as the pandemonium inside the locker room shook the walls.

With a fresh AFC North champions hat on his head, he listened as the first question came his way, a standard starter about what it feels like to be division champions, snap the Chiefs' eight-game win streak and clinch his team's first playoff berth in six seasons.

The head coach who spent the past three years offering thorough, winding answers to nearly every question thrown his way sat in silence.

Only the booming of the bass and hollering of his players filled the air.

"Very proud," Taylor managed to sneak out as emotion overcame him.

As for why this is so emotional for him, he succinctly summed up the feelings of many Bengals fans who likely shed tears of their own after the most impactful victory in the history of Paul Brown Stadium.

All that was missing was a projection screen behind him rolling the lowlights of a 6-25-1 record in his first two seasons.

"You guys have sat in here and seen what we've been through," he said.

Not just these coaches and players, but this organization, and, specifically, this city. There's always been a thought in these most significant moments, these potentially franchise-altering games, that the other shoe will drop. Bengals moments. Only pain fills these voids. That's the way life always felt for the team with the longest playoff win drought in North American professional sports.

Now they have Joe Burrow.

There's no describing what that means.

"No, you can't," Taylor said. "I don't think anyone can. We had expectations for him, and so far, he's exceeded those expectations. And, of course, he's got championships on the brain."

Now, because of Burrow, the Bengals do, too.

He threw for 446 yards, four touchdowns and no interceptions against the Chiefs, who hadn't allowed a 300-yard passer in nearly three months. He did it while taking four more sacks, hobbling between drives with a right knee injury and wearing a jersey with his nameplate ripped off.

He did it one week after posting 525 yards passing and four touchdowns against the Ravens for the fourth-most passing yards in a game in NFL history.

Nobody was talking about a battered opposing secondary this week. They instead could only talk about a monumental win, a worst-to-first culmination and the connection between Burrow and Ja'Marr Chase that removed any doubt about a team that has felt far different from its history all season.

The Bengals are real Super Bowl contenders.

"I said it in the preseason," Burrow said. "We were talking about playoffs, and I said that if we were going to go to the playoffs, the easiest way to do that was to win the division. Everyone kind of laughed at us a little bit, but we knew what kind of team we had."

Burrow has a way of removing the laughter from the situation. He's changed the conversation at every stop.

Burrow built a legend on the big stage at LSU. The brighter the lights, the more incredibly he played, the more confidence he oozed.

He's about to reach his first grand stage in the NFL. The Bengals and NFL world can only wonder what he'll do next.

As if he hasn't already done enough. He just went toe-to-toe with Patrick Mahomes, trailing by two touchdowns in January, and came out on top. Mahomes was 33-2 for his career when leading a game by at least 14 at any point.

The ability of the quarterback to pull off that feat is the bass groove of the party shaking the walls of the home locker room. It resonates inside every striped helmet.

"I think there's just a lot of emotion on this team coming together to be the 2021 Bengals. And you hear it," Taylor said, pointing to the party coming through the walls. "That's what we're about this year — love each other, believe in each other, and now we're division champs together."

How much has Burrow changed the perception of and the belief in this team? When the Bengals host whomever in the first round of the playoffs in two weeks, will fans be bemoaning the playoff win drought and assuming the worst as they run through memories of each of the seven playoff losses since Jan. 6, 1991?

No. They won't. Nor should they. They will feel like they did walking out Sunday. They'll have visual proof to always believe in Burrow, then quickly head to Joe Mixon's Instagram account to watch videos of him dancing with a cigar in his mouth, surrounded by brash teammates doing the same.

Yes, this team and its future feel far different.

"We've gotten to this point so many times and failed to capitalize," said Sam Hubbard, the Cincinnati native who grew up hearing the jokes and watching the failures. "That's kind of the narrative that's been the Cincinnati Bengals. To get an opportunity to clinch the division and actually take advantage of it and have this momentum going into the playoffs, it's something that's uncharacteristic of the Bengals and it signifies what we've been talking about for a while — about how things are changing and the direction we're heading as a franchise and as a team. It's really special."

The foundation of special starts with the connection between Burrow and Chase. When the Bengals were down 14-0 in the first quarter, it felt like it would be the latest opportunity the franchise would squander. Visions of a bitter game for their playoff lives in Cleveland next week were already conjured.

Then Chase took an 11-yard speed out, cut and accelerated through seemingly the entire Chiefs roster, reaching almost 22 mph and creating a wave of momentum that indicated the Bengals wouldn't be going quietly. That play and his special skill reminded everyone why this team looks different.

You can't coach those swings. You can only draft them (instead of Penei Sewell).

"That's just Ja'Marr Chase being Ja'Marr Chase," Taylor said. "And it really did catapult us because the momentum really was not in our favor."

By the time the dust settled on two more touchdowns, 266 yards and an incredible game-saving third-and-27 conversion down the sideline, Chase found himself doing what he said he would do on draft night in April when the dream of this Sunday was first launched.

He said then he would break all the Bengals receiving records. On Sunday, he snapped Chad Johnson's franchise record for most yards in a game and now holds the NFL record for most receiving yards in a game by a rookie.

He had more yards receiving than Patrick Mahomes did passing (259).

"Did I?" Chase said in disbelief. "What did he have? I don't think I did that. I did? Oh, shit. Sorry. Excuse my profanity. That's crazy."

Not as crazy as the latest phase in the Bengals' reconstruction finishing on Sunday. We didn't know if we would see this young group take this step this season. They'd built the foundation for a bright future. They'd created a culture that suggested things were different. They'd made shrewd moves in free agency and the draft that removed the stink of the previous two years. They'd even proved capable of toppling the perennial powers of the division.

But we still didn't know if they could contend for a Super Bowl this season. We didn't know if they were there yet.

With Evan McPherson's 20-yard field goal Sunday afternoon, the Bengals toppled the reigning king of the conference.

"We just won the AFC North," Chase said. "We're champions right now. We can go as far as we want."

The Bengals enter the playoffs with Burrow playing the best football of his life, growing into a superstar and MVP candidate right before our eyes just 26 games into his career.

We know now. This team can make a real run.

"Everything is overwhelming at the moment," Chase said. "I'm not going to lie."

Hubbard said a member of the organization told him owner Mike Brown had tears in his eyes after the game. Taylor couldn't even start his news conference without thoughts of starting his coaching career 0-11 and just wanting to see his vision get a real chance to come to light. The entire thrust of the front office, from new uniforms to investments in game days and the Ring of Honor, has been about finding a way to reconnect with the fans.

Burrow brought it all.

We'll now all find out what he brings next. Who knows? It might just end up happening in Los Angeles.

"He's not just a guy winning big regular-season games," Taylor said. "I know that's why he's here — he's always playing for championships. He's playing for championships in high school, he played for championships in college, and his expectation has always been to compete for championships here. And it's not going to be easy — we've got a lot to work to do — we're not even close yet to doing all these great things. Certainly, a big step in the right direction today, and there's no question that Joe is at the forefront of leadership on this team, and this team jumps on his back, and he'll carry us as far as we let him." ▬▬

'He Wants to Take Your Freaking Soul'

How Joe Burrow's Personality Fast-Tracked a Bengals Renaissance

January 12, 2022

BY PAUL DEHNER JR.

The tape can be slowed down, sped up, progressions and audibles explained. Throws can be analyzed for precision, tracked for accuracy to the decimal point.

Joe Burrow's emergence as a quarterback in his second season can be specifically quantified by league-leading numbers and even compared across generations.

What's made him a generational talent for the Bengals, however, and hit fast-forward on a Bengals franchise renaissance doesn't come with a Pro Football Focus grade or NextGen Stats.

"It's rare what he has," head coach Zac Taylor said. "It's hard to describe. That's the best way to put it. It's hard to describe. You have to experience the full scope of it to really understand it."

Yes, "it."

Often used, rarely explained.

Those who experienced the galvanizing, uniting force of Burrow off the field in Cincinnati mostly agree there's an intangible aura about the quarterback that captured hearts and created a team thriving in his image en route to a worst-to-first AFC North title.

They attempt to paint a picture of their quarterback's profound impact off the field, one he used to inspire a national championship at LSU in such a way that it's the stuff of legend in Baton Rouge.

There's Joe the chameleon, Joe the communicator and Joe the silently stewing. Then Joe the quiet, Joe the grinder and Joe the engine of swaggering competitiveness.

"All the confidence and the smirking, he wants to take your freaking soul," offensive coordinator Brian Callahan said. "People feel that."

Do they ever.

In Cincinnati, the upstart Bengals fed off his natural relationship-building instincts, and after just two years, he made a locker room believe they — yes, the Bengals, of all teams — are capable of making history and winning the Super Bowl.

"It is infectious," center Trey Hopkins said. "He walks around like, 'Hey, I'm about to kick your ass and I'm going to have fun.' That's what you want. Everybody in the building wants to feel like that. Everybody wants to get on board with that person."

'He has a knack for knowing what is needed'

Many memes and videos were created and circulated in the aftermath of the Bengals' 34-31 victory against Kansas City to win the North Division and clinch a playoff spot.

One stood out.

It showed four pictures side by side, of Burrow celebrating in a different way with different groups of players in the locker room.

"I thought that was the funniest thing I've seen, and I laughed my ass off," Callahan said.

While funny, it was also indicative of the most notable aspect of Burrow as a leader in the locker room. He's found a unique connection with pretty much everyone. He's a social chameleon.

"He has a relationship with every single person on the team, has a conversation with them," backup quarterback Brandon Allen said. "He's a personable type of guy and gets to know his teammates. Defensive guys go up and talk to Joe. Offensive guys go up and talk to Joe. I think that kind of feeds into that leadership role."

Burrow plays chess with Chidobe Awuzie and bought G-Shock watches for his offensive linemen. He dances with Joe Mixon on the field and recruits Riley Reiff at The Precinct. He called special teamer Stanley Morgan "everyone's favorite player on the team." When Ja'Marr Chase went through his struggles in the preseason, Burrow always stood in his corner publicly and privately.

"I try to do a lot of different things, be a lot of different people within the locker room," Burrow said. "Try to be relatable to everybody. And then nobody's going to listen to you if you don't go out and do your job and put in the work to execute on Sundays."

You won't find Burrow giving speeches often. They've happened but are more outlier than a regular occurrence.

"He's vocal at the right times," assistant coach Mark Duffner said. "It's not a monotonous record. That's a gift he has."

Through the eyes of 13-year veteran punter Kevin Huber, Burrow's voice is effective through the individual relationships, not some passionate diatribe. Huber can't help but notice how subtle, yet impactful the style proves to be.

"He has such a great feeling for what's needed at any given point," Huber said. "If the guy just needs to be talked to, you see him talk to the guy. If he needs to be pumped up, he'll pump the guy up. Someone needs encouragement, he's encouraging the guy. It's more so he has that knack for knowing what is needed in a situation."

What impressed 32-year-old veteran Mike Daniels about Burrow's evolution as a leader in their two years together was Burrow never tried to be anything he wasn't last season. He treated everyone the same in a way Daniels compared to his former MVP quarterback in Green Bay Aaron Rodgers, but what stuck out was he didn't enter with a bulldozing desire to take over the locker room.

"You automatically respect that out of the No. 1 overall pick," Daniels said. "You respect that because you expect something else out of a guy that goes that high."

Burrow instead saw Geno Atkins, A.J. Green, Carlos Dunlap, Giovani Bernard and other veterans already in place. Yeah, he was the top pick. Yeah, he was already on every billboard. Yeah, he was instantly the face of the franchise. But even as a rookie, he could read the room as well as he could read the defense.

When the old guard dispersed this offseason, Burrow admittedly assumed a natural ascension.

"I feel like I've proven myself to the team and to the league that I've earned the right to kind of speak up a little more," Burrow said.

Burrow understood the right to a voice had to be earned, even for someone dubbed savior the night he was drafted.

"He's got such an innate ability to understand human interaction and human dynamics," Callahan said. "There's nothing about it that's forced. There's nothing about it that's awkward. I've been around other guys that, they can be awkward. And they can come across as kind of phony. It's just not natural for them. His ability to relate to people is natural. And they all love him."

'He just sits there and stares'

Tight end C.J. Uzomah straightens his mouth and lifts his eyebrow. He's attempting an impression of a mad Joe Burrow.

"He'll give you a look," Uzomah said. "I've gotten the look before. You don't want that look."

Uzomah has pulled out Burrow impressions before. They all require subtlety. None more than explaining how the quarterback manifests his frustrations. It doesn't happen often so recognizing it requires much time spent.

"He'll take a deep breath," Callahan said. "Like a very deep breath. To some degree, it's his way of telling everybody. But he kind of clenches his jaw and he kind of keeps it. It's like he's like bottling it, whatever it is, as opposed to lashing out. But those guys always seem to know when he's really irritated."

For those who run a wrong route or miss an assignment, the expression of falling short of the standard doesn't come with stern words or a calculated scene of dirt kicking.

"It's a feeling, it's not words," Taylor said. "It's a brief, half-second something. Just that somebody should have done better."

Those looks or breaths happen in the moment: during practice, during a game, during a meeting. The accumulation of moments over the course of a bad practice or game, however, creates a very different view of anger.

"He doesn't show anger," Hopkins said. "It shows as focus."

The demand for better turns inward.

"You notice it if it's a bad practice," Huber said. "You will just see him sitting there in his locker and he's just, yeah, you are not going to go around him. He just sits there and stares. You can tell he's just going through it and almost doing mental reps to make sure it's not going to happen again. Him pissed off is just an internal battle with himself to make sure that never happens again."

What evolves out of this internal battle is one of the most noted aspects of Burrow's leadership skill set repeated by nearly all those who interact with him. The clear, precise communication in corrections and expectations make executing what the quarterback wants easier on game days.

"It's not a rebuke, it's an actual correction," Hopkins said. "Just, 'Hey, on this, I'm going to need you to do this.' It's very quick, to the point, fix the problem and move on."

This shows up notably with Burrow's trio of receivers, or "the athletic freakshows," as he dubbed them on Tuesday. When pointing to the dramatic improvement of the passing game during the year, the precise corrections can equate to big plays.

Callahan specifically mentions a deep bench route Tee Higgins caught against Cover 2 against San Francisco. Burrow spoke all week about how that route against a cloud coverage would need to be run deeper and let Burrow bring the route back with the throw, if necessary. Higgins kept the perfect angle and Burrow hit him for a 27-yard gain to the sideline to set up one of two drives that tied the score in regulation.

"When stuff hits the fan or something isn't quite going the way you anticipated," said Uzomah, who has repeatedly this season called Burrow the smartest player on the field, "he's able to make adjustments, sit us down and just say, 'Just do this.'"

This happens often.

"He's very direct with the receivers about what he expects," Callahan said, "which is where they probably respect him the most."

'He's eager for the fight'

Taylor will walk through the facility when he arrives on home game days and past the indoor turf field connected to the weight room.

Like clockwork, he'll see Burrow, going through his routine.

"He's not around anyone," Taylor said. "No one's really watching. But every single Sunday I've been in there since I've been here, I see a process that starts very early in the morning, and he's very consistent with it. He's not a guy who's just about the attention and does things in the limelight so that everybody sees and writes about it. He does it behind closed doors when no one's watching, when very few see it."

Even if other coaches and players don't see it, they hear about it. They feel it.

Burrow talks about understanding the need to set a tone for the entire team. When in the team facility, that's nearly always a serious one. He's about business. He's about the work. Consequently, so is everyone else.

"When you feel him come in a room and see how locked in he gets," Taylor said, "what choice do you have but to follow suit?"

What teammates are following is maniacal competitiveness. You hear this about the great players. They're wired differently. In the eyes of players, Burrow's wires are exposed for all to see from the moment you meet him.

"It can be something simple like ping-pong or football or anything," Allen said. "You can just tell he's got that competitive edge where he wants to win in everything he does. I saw that early."

Awuzie arrived as a relatively seasoned chess player, and Burrow has taken to the game to the point that a board sits in front of his locker. Awuzie won both times they played, but the seriousness on Burrow's face discussing it shows the cornerback pushed a button.

"I had to get a little better from the first one. And then I started puttin' a little pressure on him," Burrow said, then dropping the confident look he's flashed notably over the years. "I think the next game we have might be a little different."

Beating Burrow twice puts the quarterback in his comfort zone. This is how Bengals players view

him as special and what's translated so directly to why this group believes.

Whether getting recruited from a small school in Athens or having to transfer from Ohio State or willing LSU out of the shadows to one the greatest seasons in college football history and the No.1 overall pick.

The steeper the climb, the bolder the confidence.

"He's eager for the fight," Hopkins said. "He enjoys it. That's who you want to play with. The guy who looks for the hardships, looks for the problems just because he knows he can fix it. I love it."

A video circulated from Burrow's early days as a no-name, young backup for the Buckeyes. He's in a tire wrestling match against a bigger, stronger teammate. As the battle ensues, you see the edge that draws people to him.

"That type of mentality and what he did," Callahan said, "that's how he earned everybody's respect everywhere he's ever been."

In Cincinnati, the tire pull was a rookie season filled with punishment and the ultimate, gnarly knee injury. He was sacked 51 times this season, played through a dislocated pinky, hobbled with a banged-up right knee that took him off the field for the final seconds of the win over the Chiefs.

"He's tougher than hell," Duffner said. "He could play middle linebacker in a minute."

Oh yeah, all of this after an offseason of rehab from the torn ACL and MCL featuring a return at OTAs, participating in all of training camp and playing the opener against Minnesota. Being there — understanding the message his presence sent — mattered.

"Some people are more verbal with things and some people just go out there and have a stone-cold killer look and just deliver," Uzomah said. "Joe's leadership just comes with how tough he is.

You guys only see a fraction of it."

Uzomah's first impression of Burrow was of that look after a wild comeback on "Thursday Night Football" against Jacksonville. He held the straight face for five seconds in the postgame news conference that night. It came moments after Burrow threw the game-defining pass to the tight end against a zero blitz to set up Evan McPherson's field goal at the gun. He was mic'd up by NFL Films and caught screaming, "You can't zero me!" on his way off the field.

"You saw it in mic'd up against Jacksonville, you feel the energy he brings," Allen said. "It kind of goes back to the competitiveness. 'Hey, we are going to win.' People just feed off that competitiveness that he brings to the offense. It doesn't matter the score. We always believe we are going to win the game, and Joe brings that energy."

'It's been a beautiful thing to observe'

On the outside, it can look cocky. The subtle shots at Wink Martindale after launching bombs in a blowout of the Ravens while throwing for 525 yards. The mic'd-up moments. The cigars.

"He's unapologetically himself," Callahan said. "He doesn't bend or change."

The line between cocky and confident is separated by the work. His focus and level of attention at the team facility each day keep the message grounded.

"That's a big part of the quarterback position is setting the tone for the week, trying to create a narrative for the week about how you think the game is going to go, and being a positive influence in that locker room," Burrow said. "The quarterback has a lot to go into it. It's not just everything you see on the field."

These aren't impossible balances to strike. The greats do it. What's remarkable is he's doing it in only his second season.

"I'm not here to canonize him, but doggone it, he's a pretty impressive cat," Duffner said. "It has nothing to do with all the yards and that type of thing. It's not only his play. It's his mind, his toughness, competitiveness, his work ethic. All these things are clearly watched by everybody and his teammates. They clearly know, this cat's got it. It's been a beautiful thing to observe."

Now, as the Bengals face their tallest task yet in ending the 31-year playoff win drought and the pressure heightens, a sense of calm and confidence hovers over the team.

It might be hard to describe, but the dramatic flip in the belief of the franchise is no coincidence. Attitude reflects leadership.

"We have great leadership in a lot of different places," Callahan said, "but he's the face of it all."

Survive and Advance

Joe Burrow Powers Through Beating, Leads Bengals to Historic Berth in AFC Championship Game

By Jay Morrison

JANUARY 23, 2022

Joe Burrow was wearing the No. 9 long before he arrived in Cincinnati, but he never wore nine the way he did Saturday afternoon in Nashville, absorbing that many sacks.

No one has.

We've seen quarterbacks top 500 passing yards in a playoff game. We've seen them throw six touchdown passes. We've even seen them achieve perfection with a 158.3 passer rating.

But never in NFL history had we seen a quarterback take nine sacks and still lead his team to a win in the playoffs until Burrow pulled it off at Nissan Stadium, repeatedly lifting himself off the turf to help carry the Bengals to a 19-16 divisional-round victory against the AFC's No. 1 seed.

"This one was really, really hard, intense game," Burrow said.

"He's the toughest guy in the league," Bengals defensive tackle D.J. Reader said. "Just gritty. Love it. I love that about him. He's a super tough guy. He doesn't complain. Goes out there does his job. I really appreciate Joe."

It wasn't just the nine sacks. Burrow got rocked four other times after getting the pass off, and he took another shot when he scrambled 7 yards for a first down at the Tennessee 16. His headfirst dive ended with Titans safety Kevin Byard crashing into him with a knee to the back. Burrow slammed his right hand on the turf, dragged himself to his feet and, with a clump of turf wedged in his helmet, calmly and Joe Cool-y signaled his accomplishment with a simple first down point.

On the next play, running back Joe Mixon headed off right guard, cut once back to the middle, then cut again to get to the left edge, where he found nothing but space for the Bengals' only touchdown.

That play doesn't happen without Burrow selling out and taking another shot.

"Man, that boy Joey B, he's a bad man," Mixon said.

Burrow was sacked on his first snap of the game, and the assault continued unabated until his final snap, when 305-pound defensive tackle Jeffery Simmons landed on him after Burrow slid down for a 2-yard loss to put Evan McPherson on the right hash for his winning field goal.

He was sacked at least once on seven of 11 drives. Two of the ones on which he wasn't were the one-play possession when the ball went off Samaje Perine's hand for an interception — Burrow's first in six games and 209 attempts — and the final drive when he threw one pass and gave one handoff.

The Titans sacked Burrow once on each of his first three drives and five times on the first five.

"I feel good," Burrow said after the game. "Tomorrow morning might be a different story, but right now I feel great."

The nine sacks were a season high for the Titans and a career high for Burrow at any level, and they tied the NFL record for a postseason game. The Tennessee franchise was on the receiving end the only other time it has happened, when the Chiefs sacked Oilers quarterback Warren Moon nine times in a 28-20 win in the divisional round.

But despite all the rattling hits and concerning limps Burrow took, there he was, still standing and staring down the pressure. He beat a blitz to hit Ja'Marr Chase with a perfect pass on a 19-yard bench route with 15 seconds remaining to give McPherson the opportunity to send the team to the AFC Championship Game for the first time in 33 seasons.

"(The offensive line) had a great pocket for me. That was the key to that play," Burrow said, splashing praise on the group responsible for his having to unravel himself from a crumpled heap over and over again.

"(The Titans) had a great rush plan," he added. "They made it tough on us, made it tough on me, disguising coverages and blitzes and everything. They switched it up the whole game. If one thing didn't work, they moved on to the next thing, and that kept us on our toes."

Or, in Burrow's case, off them.

But as we saw in the regular season, when he was sacked a league-high 51 times, Burrow doesn't get rattled mentally, and he doesn't fold physically. Only three of the nine sacks came on third down. After the other six, Burrow dropped back to pass on the next very snap and went 6-for-6 for 52 yards.

Four of the sacks came on drives that ended in points.

Asked how Burrow was able to overcome the sacks over and over again, Bengals head coach Zac Taylor basically mimed the shrug emoji.

"If I had the answer for why Joe Burrow is good at what he does, then I don't know, I'd bottle it up and sell it," Taylor said. "He's just special. That allows us to continue to call things the way we call because even after a sack or a negative play, you still feel like we're always going to get it back. With the weapons we've got, Joe's ability to put a hit behind him and move on to the next play and find one of his freak shows, as he likes to call them, makes our job a lot easier as play callers."

Sounds as though the Comeback Player of the Year award would suit Burrow for multiple reasons.

His unflappable nature is not only impressive but also contagious. And McPherson has caught it. While so many of his teammates were lauding him in the postgame news conferences, Burrow was raving about the rookie kicker who moved into a tie for eighth place for the most field goals in a single postseason, with eight.

"That guy is unbelievable," Burrow said. "He was talking to Brandon (Allen) as he was going out to kick, and he gave a little warmup swing and he said, 'Ah, it looks like we're going to the AFC Championship,' right before he went out there and kicked it."

If that doesn't sound like a Burrow clone.

McPherson needs three more to move into sole possession of second place and six to tie Adam Vinatieri's record of 14, set in 2006.

"We knew exactly what we had as soon as he walked into the building in camp, and we just saw how he carried himself," Burrow said. "You know exactly how a kicker is going to perform when obviously everyone at this level can kick through the uprights, but it's how you handle yourself in the locker room that shows us that you have the confidence to go out there and make a kick like this and perform the way he did in a game like this. We knew exactly what kind of guy we had in camp."

The sentiment was the same about Burrow when he showed up as a rookie. Since then, he's been sacked multiple times in 22 of his 28 starts, along with a devastating non-sack that shredded his left knee.

It's hard to gauge what's more amazing — that the Bengals are in the AFC Championship Game with an offensive line that has allowed multiple sacks in 12 consecutive games and 66 in the 19 contests this season, or what their ceiling can be if and when they finally fix it.

Not all of the sacks were the fault of the offensive line Saturday. Burrow held the ball too long on a few occasions, two of which were the can't-happen types where he took the team out of field goal range.

But regardless of where the blame belonged, the response was almost always the same. Burrow found a way to overcome the negative and carry the Bengals to new heights with their first road playoff victory in franchise history.

When cornerback Eli Apple broke up a Ryan Tannehill pass near midfield and linebacker Logan Wilson plucked the ball out of the air to give Burrow 20 seconds to move the Bengals close enough for McPherson, no one on the Cincinnati sideline had any doubt about what was coming.

"He does it time and time again," Mixon said of Burrow. "Poise under pressure. And I'm just so happy for him because of all the work that he put in his offseason, getting his leg right, working on his arm and building his body up so he could take whatever happens to him. He got sacked a couple times. We've got to clean that up. But by him overcoming all that he's been through, I just can't do nothing but say that I'm proud of that man." ▬▬

'He Just Finds a Way'

Joe Burrow's Confidence, Determination, Elusiveness Lead Bengals to Super Bowl

By Jay Morrison

JANUARY 30, 2022

Joe Burrow has as much confidence and belief in himself and his teammates as anyone in the Bengals organization. Maybe more than anyone on the face of the Earth. But five months ago, not even Burrow thought the events that played out Sunday afternoon at Arrowhead Stadium, with the Bengals rallying from an 18-point deficit to beat the Chiefs 27-24 in overtime of the AFC Championship Game, were within the realm of rational thought.

"I think if you would've told me before the season started that we'd be going to the Super Bowl, I probably would've called you crazy," Burrow said. "I think if you would've told me coming into the league, when I got drafted, that we would be here this year, it would be a shock."

But on the 21st Sunday in a season full of rapid-fire growth, record-breaking performances, resiliency and resolve, Burrow would have called you crazy if you told him the Bengals weren't going to the Super Bowl.

Even when the Chiefs scored their third touchdown in three possessions to take a 21-3 lead with five minutes in the first half.

Even when the home team had first-and-goal at the 1-yard line with a chance to boost the lead back to 18 going in the final seconds before halftime.

Even when Kansas City was 5 yards and four plays away from scoring the go-ahead touchdown with 90 seconds left in regulation.

Even when the Chiefs won the overtime coin toss and a repeat of last week's divisional win against the Bills felt like an inevitability to anyone even remotely familiar with Patrick Mahomes.

Burrow thrives on doubt. He embraces the arduous. He's 6-0 this year when the Bengals were underdogs of three or more points (vs Vikings +3; at Ravens +6.5; at Broncos +3; vs Chiefs +3.5; at Titans +4; at Chiefs +7).

He's probably pissed they didn't trail by 19 instead of 18 on Sunday so he could have helped set an NFL record for the largest comeback in a conference championship game. The Bengals instead will have to share it with the 2006 Colts, who also fell behind 21-3 before rallying to beat the Patriots 38-34.

But while the Colts did it at home, Burrow and the Bengals did it on Everest, conquering one of the loudest venues in America while toppling a team playing in its fourth consecutive AFC Championship Game and looking for its third straight Super Bowl trip.

"I don't know if you ever want to get down 21-3," Burrow said. "I said it earlier in the year when we started making some of these comebacks, I never really feel like we're out of it. But obviously, 21-3 isn't exactly the most exciting position to be in."

But it's not exactly the direst either, not with Burrow running the show.

This was the third time this year the Bengals rallied from a deficit of at least 14 points to win. The Bengals as a franchise had only done it 13 times in their first 53 seasons of existence.

They trailed the Jaguars by 14 in Week 4, and Burrow threw for 253 yards and two touchdowns in the second half of a 24-21 victory.

They trailed this same Chiefs team by 14 just four weeks ago, and Burrow again threw for 253 yards and two touchdowns in the second half as part of a 466-yard performance and a division-clinching 34-31 win.

But this wasn't that, with Burrow putting the team on his shoulders and compiling huge numbers to race past a team searching for answers.

It was Burrow searching for solutions, ad-libbing, looking for escape routes.

"He just finds a way to make plays when there isn't a play to be made," head coach Zac Taylor said. "It makes my life much easier. It doesn't have to be the perfect play call, he is going to figure it out. I probably called one of his all-time favorite plays in the third quarter and it did not work at all. He scrambled and found Ja'Marr (Chase) coming across the field for a scramble play. That is his bread and butter. It was a disaster. The coverage took everyone away. They blitzed us. There was nothing there, and Joe figured it out. I am just really proud of the effort he had today and putting us in this position."

On the play Taylor was referencing, the Bengals still were staring at the 11-point deficit they carried into halftime. It was second-and-10 at their own 46-yard line. The Chiefs sent six pass rushers. Burrow slid left and found two of them staring him in the face. Defensive tackle Chris Jones got his left arm around the waist, but Burrow slithered free it. Jones had his right arm wrapped around the left calf as he fell to the ground, but Burrow mule-kicked out of it, took off running to his right and delivered a Mahomes-esque pass, releasing the ball with neither foot on the ground.

The 22-yard pass to Chase put the Bengals in field goal range, and Evan McPherson ended up hitting his second of four to inch the team a little closer at 21-13.

Settling for field goals is not going to beat the Chiefs on most days. It worked Sunday because of the Bengals defense. Its performance — Eli Apple's tackle of Tyreek Hill at the 1-yard line on the final play of the first half; B.J. Hill's interception in the third quarter; Vonn Bell's pick in overtime; Sam Hubbard's back-to-back sacks when the Chiefs had second-and-goal at the 4 with 1:26

remaining; three points allowed in the second half; eight straight possessions without allowing a touchdown; holding the Chiefs to 2-of-8 on third down after halftime — was greater and more impactful in many ways than Burrow's.

He completed 23 of 38 passes for 250 yards and two touchdowns with one interception. His 6.6 yards per attempt were his second-fewest of the season. His 60.5 completion percentage was tied for second-lowest.

But when a play had to be made, Burrow got it done, by land or air.

"When the game is on the line, he is going to figure it out," Taylor said. "Whether it is with his feet or extending plays. He made a comment last night that he was going to rush for 100 yards. I don't know how many he ran for, but he sure took off there in the fourth quarter. He made some huge plays with his feet."

There was a third-and-1 quarterback sneak two plays before he double-juked Jones to hit Chase.

There was the third-and-goal touchdown pass to Chase one series later to convert Hill's interception and get the Bengals within 21-19 with 2:18 left in the third, followed by the two-point pass to Trent Taylor to tie the game.

There was third-and-6 from the Cincinnati 24, when Jones looked as though he might rip Burrow's nameplate off the second game in a row, only to have the quarterback duck out of it. Then with Jones in pursuit, Burrow appeared to slow down, waiting for Jones to dive at his legs before high-step accelerating away from trouble.

"He is not geared to run around," Chiefs safety Tyrann Mathieu said. "He is not geared to get 60 to 70 rushing yards a game. I think he is a smart player, a smart quarterback. Hats off to him. Obviously, this kid studies a lot of tape. He has the instincts to go with it as well, and he made a couple of third-down scrambles today that lifted their team. Anytime you can get off the field when it is third-and-6 or third-and-7, third-and-long, you have to dig deep and try your best to get off the field. It just felt like those guys made a little bit more plays than us today."

Three plays after getting away from Jones, Burrow was facing third-and-7. The Chiefs only rushed four and had all the receivers covered. Burrow tucked the ball and raced up the middle off the field for an 11-yard gain and another first down that came with a shot from cornerback Rashad Fenton when Burrow declined to slide. A facemask also went uncalled on the play.

Burrow didn't come close to 100 yards rushing, but he had 28 — the third-highest of his career — before intentionally losing three on his final snap, setting up McPherson on the right hash for his game-winning, Super Bowl-sending field goal.

"He is a great quarterback who executed on every cylinder to get his team to the Super Bowl," Chiefs defensive end Frank Clark said. "The guy can get sacked last week eight or nine times and he goes out and wins the game. Even when we played him the first time around, we sacked him four times and some good hits and he stands back up, calls a play and (goes and) wins the game. Hats off to him. Young guy, great quarterback. He is going to win a lot of football games in this league."

Those back-to-back first-down rushes got the Bengals close enough for a McPherson 52-yard field goal that put them up 24-21 with 6:07 to go.

But after the Chiefs tied it on a field goal at the end of regulation and won the overtime coin toss, Burrow couldn't do anything but watch and hope the defense would put the ball back in his hands.

And when it did with Jessie Bates deflecting a Mahomes deep ball to Bell, Burrow wasn't going to give it back.

He knew it, and so did every one of his teammates.

"My heart rate didn't raise," Hubbard said. "I had all the confidence in the world that after we got that turnover by Vonn Bell, we were going to take care of the ball and march down the field. We have the most reliable kicker in the NFL, ice it off if we weren't going to score. I knew once we got that first stop, it was in Joe's hands and we're good."

He was talking about the final possession of overtime, but he might as well be talking about the future.

The Bengals are in Burrow's hands. They're good.

No matter what happens in the years to come, it will never feel like it did Sunday. Expectations will grow, and Super Bowl absences, not appearances, will seem crazy.

But for now, the party rages.

It's exactly what the Bengals had in mind when they drafted Burrow No. 1 just 647 days ago. The way Sunday played out may not have been what they had in mind, but that's what makes Burrow special. One way or another, he wins.

"I've been pretty miserable along with my teammates for the last few years, losing so many games," Hubbard said. "I told Joe, 'We need you. You're the guy to turn this around. I know it.' He embraced that. What are the odds that a kid from Athens, Ohio, is a national champion, Heisman Trophy winner, prime to be the No. 1 overall pick and we happen to have it? You can't even write stories like this. It's amazing."

Amazing, not crazy. ▰▰

BUILDING A LEGACY

Icon in the Making

Joe Burrow is Shining On and Off the Field

By Jon Greenberg

FEBRUARY 8, 2022

Micah Saltzman was in Athens, Ohio, scrolling Instagram when he saw his direct messages light up. In his inbox was a post of Joe Burrow wearing Saltzman's heart-emblazoned sherpa jacket while walking into the biggest game of his professional football career.

"It was a full-on surprise, for sure," Saltzman said.

Complete with rimless "buffs" sunglasses, a black turtleneck and an iced-out pendant on his neck, it was a look that exuded confidence — if nothing else.

Saltzman, a 21-year-old budding model/fashion designer, had sent Burrow, his older brother Zacciah's close friend, a box of his new designs before the season.

Burrow waited until the AFC Championship, when all eyes were on him, to unveil the jacket to the world. And he wanted it to be a surprise.

"Last week, he hit me up and he's like, 'Yo, don't tell your brother, so it'll be a surprise, but have you seen the jacket he just made? That shit's sick,'" Zacciah said. "He said, 'It's not even because it's your brother. I just really like the design.'"

"That was very generous of him," Micah said.

The jacket went viral, and Saltzman's streetwear-inspired brand Live2Love got an influx of orders, particularly after a GQ writer delved into Burrow's newfound trendsetter status and linked to the website. Now Saltzman is taking pre-orders on a coat that he designed on his iPad in Athens, Ohio.

It's not the first time Burrow has surprised someone by wearing their design. At a Nov. 28 game, he wore a Bengals-themed BlaCk OWned Outerwear satin bomber jacket to a game. He had offered to do it during his rookie season, but he tore his ACL before it could happen.

"We had no idea that Burrow was going to wear that jacket on that day," BlaCk OWned Outerwear CEO Means Cameron told *The Athletic's* Rhiannon Walker. "In fact, it wasn't on our mind, he just popped up. Someone said, 'Hey, you catch ESPN?' And then we saw it."

By making the Super Bowl in his second year in the league, Burrow, a national champion in college and the No. 1 pick in the 2020 NFL draft, has reached a new level of fame, one that comes with an almost unnatural degree of attention. Not since the days of Chad Ochocinco have the nuts-and-bolts-focused Bengals reporters had to endure all of these superfluous questions about high fashion.

Like it or not, when Burrow, after leading the Bengals to their first playoff victory in 31 years, wears rimless, rose-colored Cartier sunglasses (or "buffs") to the press conference, people are going to pay attention. He's not Cam Newton, challenging paradigms every game, but with his boyish looks and rock-solid confidence, Burrow can pull off a look.

"When I found us trying to find pink-tinted glasses for our staff to wear in the stores, I knew that it had reached a different level with him," said Josh Sneed, one of the co-founders of Cincy Shirts, a T-shirt company that is in the business of churning out Bengals and Burrow clothing.

Sneed and his team immediately incorporated the picture of Burrow in the glasses into a pop-art style shirt with the nickname "Joey Warhol." It's currently the company's top seller, Sneed said, "and it's not really close."

Burrow, of course, has brought the attention on himself by wearing fancy jewelry and $1,000 pink sunglasses to and from his job as the Bengals starting quarterback, where players are captured on film like they're walking a runway when they enter the stadium.

And to Burrow's credit, he's handled the additional questioning with aplomb. Some athletes bristle at the extra attention they overtly crave, but when asked if the diamonds in his chain were real after the AFC Championship, Burrow said, "I make too much money for them to be fake."

As for his newfound influencer status, "I don't really consciously think about it," Burrow said during a Monday media appearance for Super Bowl week.

"I just wear stuff I think I would like," he said. "It's not like I'm shopping and go, oh, everyone would love this. I just don't care what anybody thinks about what I wear or what I do. I just wear what I like."

The Joe Burrow wardrobe contains multitudes, from suits to streetwear. So he might wear a SpongeBob SquarePants "Krusty Krab" sweatshirt and a Santa hat to a post-game press conference. Or it might be a suit. Micah Saltzman said he heard a comparison of Burrow's style to the famous swinging days of Joe Namath, which he can see.

"He also carries himself as like a professional businessman," Saltzman said. "So the suit game is sick. I love that."

To those who have known him, Burrow's confidence in wearing whatever he wants isn't a surprise. But seeing him in the digital pages of GQ was not what people were expecting out of him.

"That blows my mind," said Trae Williams, who played with Burrow at Athens High School after transferring in when his dad got a job coaching with Joe's father Jimmy Burrow at Ohio University. "Because when I met Joe, and pretty much everybody (at Athens High), they dressed for school as they were going for a run. I saw the football part coming, but not him becoming a fashion icon."

Like a lot of fashion icons, Burrow finds his equilibrium by mixing high- and low-priced items. The sherpa jacket, which retails for $169.99, was combined with a necklace that costs much, much more. As the GQ article explained, the custom-made JB9 with a swoosh pendant was crafted by Leo Frost, a celebrity jeweler out of Houston.

"My idea behind doing that was like, you know, he's gonna be one of Nike's biggest superstars," Frost told GQ writer Eileen Carter. "He's rocking with the name Joey Ice."

"Yeah that necklace, I was surprised about that one," Joe's mother Robin said. "But I like it."

Burrow has more where that comes from. Zacciah Saltzman said Burrow has a SpongeBob pendant he's yet to unveil to the public.

Joe's parents, a retired college football coach and an elementary school principal, are still living in The Plains, a suburb of Athens, and though they raised him in his leisurewear days, they're enjoying his newfound fashionista fame, albeit for different reasons.

"I love it," Robin said. "I like that he shows his personality and isn't afraid to go out a little bit outside of the box on things. I think Jimmy has a little bit of a different perspective of that because he's a little more conservative than I am as far as fashion goes."

"Well, it's probably not something I would throw out there," Jimmy Burrow said. "He just likes to have fun with it, and I think it makes him feel good. Maybe it takes a little of the anxiety, the pressure, off thinking about the game."

Winning a national title at LSU got Burrow more than his share of street cred, digital and otherwise. It was there that he started to develop his public persona — confident but not brash, bold and likable — and important people have noticed.

"I already knew he had a lotta drip since he went to LSU," Houston rapper/jewelry designer Paul Wall wrote in a text message. "But I'm impressed with his jewelry game. He's wearing some top-quality stuff. Me and Johnny (Dang) are ready to make him some grillz to match!"

This message was passed along to Burrow through Zacciah Saltzman, who reported that Burrow's Bengals receiver and former LSU teammate, Ja'Marr Chase, already had it covered.

Everyone, it seems, has an interest in seeing Joe Burrow shine. ▬▬

Everyone Loves Joe

Why Joe Burrow is Treasured by Bulldogs and Buckeyes, Tigers and Bengals

By Jon Greenberg and Brody Miller

FEBRUARY 10, 2022

A few days after the AFC Championship game that changed his life, Joe Burrow was talking to a longtime friend on the phone. And when Burrow and Zacciah Saltzman talk, stupid jokes eventually morph into deeper dialogues. And in this conversation, as his new reality began to set in, Burrow talked about the nature of fame.

"He was like, 'I can't believe at the end of the day, I'm literally just playing football, just throwing a pigskin around, and this is what people see me as,'" Saltzman said. "He's just throwing a ball to people. And because he can do that better than other people, he's a legend."

Saltzman, who played football with Burrow at Athens High, will be at the Super Bowl in person Sunday. So will Burrow's family, some friends and coaches.

But plenty of other people will be there in spirit. Entire cities. Most of two states. The Joe Burrow diaspora.

As he's shown everywhere he plays, Joe Burrow is a uniter.

Athens is just one hometown that claims Burrow, who was born in Ames, Iowa, and spent time in Lincoln, Neb., and Fargo, N.D., before his dad Jimmy Burrow moved the family to Athens for a college football coaching job.

From high-school stardom in southeast Ohio, Joe Burrow went north to Columbus to play for the Ohio State Buckeyes, and when that didn't work out, he took his right arm (and his degree) to Baton Rouge, La., to play for the LSU Tigers. That led him back to Ohio when the Bengals took him with the No. 1 pick in the 2020 NFL Draft.

Athens, Columbus, Baton Rouge and Cincinnati are all basking in the reflected glory of Burrow, the precocious quarterback who has taken the NFL by storm with an unlikely, unbelievable Super Bowl berth.

"It's funny, because everyone wants to claim a piece," said Trae Williams, who played high school football with Burrow and Saltzman.

At LSU, for instance, the fans retain an almost religious fervor about what Burrow was able to accomplish in two seasons, culminating in a national championship.

"I do feel a bit like the chosen people, in a way. Like God's people," said T-Bob Hebert, a former LSU center who now hosts a major Baton Rouge morning radio show. "I feel like we witnessed first-hand the power of this man, and because of that, if anybody questions Joe — like go question Joe Burrow to an LSU fan, question anything, and you would get loudly shouted down."

As the starting quarterback of a Super Bowl team, Burrow has reached the precipice of sports immortality at the beginning of his NFL career.

The Bengals are decided underdogs this week in Los Angeles, facing the Rams at their home stadium. What can Burrow do against those odds and that defensive front?

To hear the people around Ohio and Louisiana talk about Joe Burrow, the man and the myth, there are no limits. Only glorious possibilities.

———————— A ————————

The curious nature of athletic celebrity is something we take for granted, why we value some jobs more than others. But for a 25-year-old, baby-faced Joe Burrow going through the transition from quarterback to Super Bowl quarterback in real time, it's weighty stuff to think about. The people who have known Burrow the longest feel that he is equipped to handle the mental load.

"He's a pretty deep guy," Saltzman said.

"Super, super confident, and he's not a jerk about it," Williams said. "But he's gonna let you know."

How popular is Burrow in Ohio? Well, if he wins his next game, he's in the neighborhood of space-traveling John Glenn and title-winning LeBron James. His comps are astronauts and kings.

Burrow's parents, Jimmy and Robin, have been dealing with their son's rising stature for the past three years. It's one thing to raise a small-town sports hero who goes into coaching or business. But now their son has the chance for a uniquely American hero trifecta: Heisman winner, college football national champion and Super Bowl winner.

And he could do it in a three-year span.

"I just continue to just say it's so surreal," Robin Burrow said in a phone conversation from her home outside of Athens. "You think that it's gotten to be as great as it's going to be, and it just keeps getting bigger and better."

Since Joe's Heisman season, Jimmy has taken on the lead role as his son's press contact and anecdote provider. He retired from his job as the defensive coordinator of Ohio University's football team to enjoy his son's senior year and found himself busier than ever.

Jimmy, who has been a football coach in college or high school since 1981, had never tailgated, but soon enough, he became a pro at it outside of Tiger Stadium. In the past two seasons, he's engrossed himself in the NFL for the first time since getting drafted by the Packers in 1976. He and Robin host a tailgate at Bengals games and welcome family and friends from all over the country to share in their experiences.

The Burrows get stopped often when they're home — Robin is the principal of Eastern Elementary School in nearby Meigs County — and when they go to Cincinnati, they're amazed at all of the

fans who revere their son. Burrow's brother, Dan, was stopped in Nashville by a Titans fan asking him to sign their Burrow jersey. At LSU, it was similar adoration with about twice as many people in attendance at the games. But the difference in Cincinnati is thousands of people are wearing the Burrow surname on their backs.

"That first game we went to this year against the Vikings, there's literally thousands of (his jerseys), and so that was kind of our first, 'Hey, this has gotten to be a pretty big thing here,'" Jimmy said. "And it's a little overwhelming at times. People want to talk about Joe everywhere we go, and we're good with that. We never get tired of talking about our son, and he just happens to be now in the Super Bowl. But it's a good thing. We enjoy it."

Burrow is only the fourth quarterback who was born in or grew up in the football-mad state of Ohio to make the Super Bowl, joining Len Dawson, Roger Staubach and Ben Roethlisberger. And though he made his college name at LSU after redshirting and backing up other quarterbacks at Ohio State, Burrow's Buckeye State bonafides are unquestioned and celebrated.

He took Athens High to the state championship game at Ohio Stadium, where they fell to Toledo Central Catholic. (During Super Bowl week, Burrow again mentioned how that loss still pains him.) His 11,428 passing yards are the fourth-highest in Ohio history, and his 156 touchdowns are the third-highest. His senior year he threw for 4,437 yards and 63 touchdowns. Athens' stadium is now named for him.

Burrow did all of this for a high school not known for its athletics success — and that's putting it nicely. But he teamed up with an unusually high number of NCAA Division I-caliber athletes who wound up playing at Ohio, Northwestern and Georgetown, not to mention his basketball teammate Ibi Watson, who went to Michigan and Dayton and now plays in the G League.

At Ohio University, current students and alumni treat Burrow with the same amount of veneration as Goodfella's Pizza or The CI.

Students aren't just wearing Burrow Bengals jerseys to the Court St. bars, they're also still wearing LSU ones. On the night of the AFC championship game, students were celebrating in the streets. There's a banner over the main drag of Uptown Athens, and every tavern is now a de facto Bengals bar. A local arts collective Passion-Works Studio (motto: To inspire and liberate the human spirit through the arts) had a Burrow- and Bengals-inspired painting night. Donkey Coffee has a drink named after him, and Bagel Street Deli (Bengal Street Deli on Twitter) has a sandwich inspired by him. If only Burrow could stop at any of these places and not get swarmed.

As his fame grew at LSU, his anonymity in Athens declined. After he won a Heisman and a national title, it became impossible.

"After the national championship game we had a little reunion back in Athens," Williams said. "We wanted to go play pool on Court St., so we went to Pawpurr's because we knew one of the bartenders there. So it was like, 'Hey man, Joe's coming in, let's keep this on the low end and not let the entire campus know. There shouldn't be that many people out there tonight, we'll be fine.' It was like 10 minutes and the entire bar is flooded and we're having to escape out the back."

Burrow wasn't one to go out during his LSU title run. He once joked as an online graduate student he only knew three locations in Baton Rouge — His apartment, a nearby shopping center and the L'Auberge Casino — with his focus purely set on winning football games. The only teammate confirmed to have gone to Burrow's place those two years was center Lloyd Cushenberry, because he lived in the same building, and Dan Burrow isn't even confident whether Joe's closest teammates Clyde Edwards-Helaire and Thaddeus Moss ever made it in.

But one time, after beating Arkansas in Tiger Stadium in 2019, Burrow wanted to entertain some friends. His former Ohio State teammates J.T. Barrett and Stephen Collier were in town, so Burrow used some connections to get in touch with the co-owner of Uncle Earl's bar, BG Lanoix. Lanoix set it up so Burrow and company could enter through the back, and Burrow kept a low profile with a hoodie and a ball cap covering his face.

The next day, the diehard LSU fan Lanoix had to check the camera footage. He saw an intoxicated LSU fan rocking a No. 9 Burrow jersey, chaotically dancing along the dance floor railing. Lanoix laughed.

The fan had no idea that two feet below him was an incognito Burrow on a rare night out.
Flash forward to this season, in the second week of November, Burrow was the quarterback of a 5-4 football team and had a week off. The Bengals had just lost to the Browns 41-16 in a game that saw Burrow throw two interceptions and zero touchdowns. With a few days free, he found himself in Columbus, his old college home, the place he had to leave to become a legend in two states.

"I was like, come on, we might as well go out," Saltzman said. "(Bengals defensive end) Sam Hubbard was there and he was like, 'What do you think about going out?' And Joe said, 'Well, No. 1, it's not a good look after losing to the Browns last week. And two, I'm not going to have a fun time in that atmosphere anyway. So there's no point.' We were all kind of like, that makes perfect sense."

So they had a quiet dinner at The Top Steak House and went back to an Airbnb that Burrow had rented.

"We watched a movie and listened to a lot of Kid Cudi," Saltzman said.

That attitude didn't change when the Bengals' fortunes did. After the Bengals beat the Chiefs in Week 17 to clinch a playoff berth, some people wanted to go out but Joe just went to Hubbard's house, where they played cards with Trey Hendrickson, DJ Reader, Hubbard and Kevin Huber. Then, after the playoff win against the Raiders, Dan got back to his little brother's house at midnight hoping to celebrate. Joe had been in bed since 9:45 p.m.

There's a difference between being a famous quarterback and being a legend. Much of it has to do with winning, which Burrow has done a remarkable job of over the past three years. But there's something else about Burrow that endears him to people in a unique way.

And if there was a moment when Burrow became more than a quarterback, it was during his Heisman Trophy acceptance speech two years ago.

Two hours before he officially won the award given to the best college player in the country, a prelude to the national championship he would win for LSU a few weeks later, Jimmy Burrow went to his son's room to see if he had anything prepared when the inevitable award was announced.

The elder Burrow found his son jotting down some notes for his speech. Joe told his dad he wasn't going to write out a formal speech. What he wound up saying changed lives. Not something you can normally say about a Heisman speech.

"Coming from southeast Ohio, it's a very impoverished area," Burrow said. "The poverty rate is almost two times the national average. There's so many people there who don't have a lot, and I'm up here for all those kids in Athens and Athens County that go home to not a lot of food on the table, hungry after school. You guys can be up here too."

He paused to collect himself, and that's when the applause started. But it hasn't ended.

"The crazy thing is I remember talking to him about it," Saltzman said. "And that was completely off-script. He was going to give a little thanks, and I think when he got up there, he really started thinking about Athens and his connection to it, and I think that just hit him so hard that he just got super emotional. He's always gonna rep the community, but I don't think he anticipated crying, you know?"

No one remembers Heisman speeches, but as the NFL is learning, Burrow is a little different.

"I mean, we knew he knew about that, and was sensitive to it, because he had friends that were not as fortunate as he was and he always treated them the same no matter what," Jimmy said. "But this wasn't really a dinner-table discussion. So, you know, he opened our eyes to that."

"Food insecurity" is defined by the charity Feeding America as "a lack of consistent access to enough food for every person in a household to live an active, healthy life." As of Feeding America's records from 2019, there were 12,460 food-insecure people in Athens County, which accounts for 18.9 percent of the population. That was one of the highest percentages in Ohio. The charity estimates that more than 38 million people face food insecurity in this country.

"It did blow everybody away, including us," Robin Burrow said. "It was so great to hear him speak of his love for our area. And for me, as a mom, I was so proud that he was so reflective and aware of all of the needs in the area and very happy that he used that platform that he had that night, to be able to bring some extra support and, and really some awareness of that problem in our area."

Will Drabold, a former journalist who was three grades ahead of Burrow at Athens High, was watching and was so moved, he wanted to use the moment to do something.

He remembered there was an Athens County Food Pantry, and he checked its Facebook page and saw it could take donations via the website. So he created a little fundraiser with a $1,000 goal and sent the link to friends and family.

"I put that up and then later that day, got on a flight from Columbus to L.A., and when I landed, it was like $25,000," he said. "So this is something. I woke up early Pacific time, it was like $80,000. I was like, 'Oh my God, this is crazy.' That was not even 48 hours after a speech."

Drabold's Facebook messages were full of support from LSU fans.

"I started getting messages from people all over Louisiana," he said. "Like we got this, the Cajuns got it."

They did get it, and so did a slew of other people. The fund became a social-media sensation, raising $650,000 by the end of January. Other fundraisers for local missions popped up as well.

Burrow made food insecurity in Appalachian Ohio a trending topic.

Karin Bright, the head of the Athens County Food Pantry, said, "It enabled us to change the model we had used for years, and that model was we had a certain amount (of food) that we packed (to give away) each week. We had our budgeted amount, and this is what we packed. And at the end of the week, if we ran out on Thursday, we ran out on Thursday. If we made it to Friday, then that was great.

"So when we knew that we no longer had to worry about that limitation, we immediately went to what we now call a never-out model. Anytime we start to run low on those packed bags and boxes, we bring in a packing crew. Whatever the demands are, we're able to meet that demand and don't have to turn anyone away because we were out of food for that week."

They wanted to divvy up and invest the money in a responsible manner and one thing they wanted to do was create a "long-term sustainable investment." They decided to partner with the Foundation for Appalachian Ohio. The food pantry donated $350,000 to get this started, which the foundation matched, and they named the fund for Burrow.

"Joe generously and graciously permitted us to use his name to name that fund," Bright said. "So that's why it's named the Joe Burrow Hunger Relief Fund, because we wanted to honor what he had said and the fact that he had put such a spotlight on hunger and food insecurity in this area."

Burrow didn't find fame in Columbus. But he still holds Ohio State true to his heart.

"I'm definitely still a Buckeye," he told reporters recently.

After all, he came to Urban Meyer's football factory with a lot to prove. He was a highly touted player with immense numbers but was not a slam-dunk Power 5 QB recruit. NFL quarterbacks don't come from the Tri-Valley Conference, no matter who their dad is.

"I really wasn't very good coming into college, and I knew that I was going to have to get better," Burrow said Monday during his first Super Bowl press conference. "I came from a really small school in high school, and it was kind of a culture shock when I got to Ohio State and realized how good everybody was. So I knew I wasn't going to play early, but I worked really hard, and they helped develop me to the player that I am today. So I owe Ohio State quite a bit."

As Tim Hall, a sports-radio host in Columbus said in a conversation, Burrow's connections to Ohio State are obvious — "He, 100%, is a Buckeye. I think it's ridiculous to say that he's not." — and fans are taking pride in his local success. But this is a fan base still waiting for an Ohio State quarterback to take hold in the NFL, and Hall doesn't think Buckeyes fans can truly lay claim to Burrow as their guy in the NFL.

"I think to this day, the best QB they've ever produced in the NFL is Mike Tomczak, and that's

shocking, Mike Tomczak for a football program as proud as Ohio State," Hall said. "They were hoping that Dwayne Haskins would be that first guy and he wasn't, so now it's Justin Fields."

This week, Homage, a popular sports apparel company based in Columbus, re-launched its "Just A Kid From Athens" shirts, with part of the proceeds going to the Southeast Ohio Food Bank. Homage was founded by an Ohio University graduate and focuses on Ohio State gear, so Burrow is a natural attraction. The company just got its NFL license in January, perfect timing to sell Bengals gear as well. Homage has been selling every orange hoodie it has and spending the week working to stock their stores in Columbus, Cleveland and Cincinnati.

"This week, there's so many stories coming out about Joe Burrow, the Ohio kid, I think our audience, our audience being Ohio State fans, a lot of Ohio State fans, there's just a lot of love for him," said Nathan Okuley, Homage's vice president of brand marketing. "So, the moment he said, 'You know, I'm still a Buckeye,' I feel like the amount of searches that we saw on our site for Joe Burrow just skyrocketed."

The football pecking order among Columbus sports fans has long been Ohio State, the Browns and then the Bengals. But things are changing.

"I think the fan base, the Cincinnati fan base, is growing louder and louder in Columbus each and every day," Okuley said. "In years past, I would say it was predominantly a Browns city, at least you know, just by walking the streets or talking to people who were going to sports bars. So I think you've seen a shift."

As Evan McPherson's kick went through the uprights in Kansas City on Jan. 30, the bars in Louisiana erupted as if it were a Saints game. This was their favorite adopted son, the Ohio transplant who changed his jersey to read "Burreaux"

on senior night to make clear this will always be his other home. The Walk-On's by Tiger Stadium, the fittingly named Bengal Tap Room and homes throughout the state cheered because he is their guy. Burrow didn't start out at LSU, but they hold him as dear as any athlete in school history.

Lanoix had 25 or so people over for that AFC title game. His dad made sauce piquante, and they drank wine as the Bengals went down 18. It could have been over, "But here comes fuckin' Burrow again," he said.

"At the end of the game, I told everyone there, 'I love the Saints, but I think people were happier and celebrating more that Joe was going to the Super Bowl than if the Saints would have won.' Maybe not that extreme, but pretty close."

The reverence Burrow draws in Louisiana is matched only by Drew Brees, the man whose Saints' Super Bowl helped a state heal after Hurricane Katrina. But Burrow carries his own unprecedented sort of folklore, this near mythological quality that makes people just believe. It goes back to Hebert referring to LSU fans as "the chosen people." Now they follow him unconditionally, leading to an entire state of southern Bengals fans.

LSU has had great players before, sure, but Burrow is something different. He's the guy who took the offense from the Stone Age and made it college football's greatest ever. He's the one who, every time LSU went down, allowed them to feel a strange sense of calm. Because they had Burrow. And he did it with his sense of cool.

"It's all very meathead, but the thing you can't get away from is the animalistic alpha sort-of aura," Hebert said. "The alpha aura. There's always gotta be a big dog. Eventually, you're going to get to the top ... It's his supreme confidence and belief in himself."

Lindsey Thompson, a Cincinnati native who has been LSU Athletics' creative services coordinator for the past five years, has the complete perspective of Burrow. She's lived the years of Bengals losing, she's lived a few years of LSU being unable to field a modern offense, and she's seen Burrow come to both places and "He just changes the world."

Thompson has spent each Bengals playoff game at the same table at Walk-On's. At first, the whole bar was casually rooting for their boy Burrow, but eventually, the place evolved into roaring fans hyping her up. On the other side of the building, a video captured LSU's new assistant athletic director of sports nutrition, a young, well-built Ohio native named Matt Frakes, succumbing to deep tears as the kick went through.

But the Burrow's reach doesn't stop with the football program. It touches Leslie Blanchard, an adjunct professor at LSU also serving as executive director of the school's Leadership Development Institute. Burrow took three graduate-level courses on leadership under Blanchard, all electives he pursued because he simply wanted to grow as a leader. She joked with him in the summer of 2019 that she wanted him to sign his final paper and send it back before he won a Heisman and a national championship.

After the season — and thanks to her new friendship with Burrow's mother — Blanchard checked her mailbox. Burrow's final paper was signed "Joey B" with the message, "Thanks for all the help."

"I won't lie to you, I fist bump the air every time a commentator or reporter says, 'This man shows such great leadership for his age.'" Blanchard said. "I'm like, 'Yeah, he does!'"

By the time LSU had become No. 1 and beaten Alabama, the Burrow clan was like LSU's first family. While tailgating the final home game, Jimmy, Joe's eldest brother Jamie and Jamie's stepson Charlie were playing catch. It was three generations of Burrow men throwing a football around before watching Joe's Heisman run.

And right then, some college kids came up and asked if they're the Burrows. They said yes.

"The next thing you know, our special moment had ended and been replaced by these college kids running routes because they wanted to catch passes from Joe's dad, Joe's brother and Joe's nephew," Jamie said.

Lanoix watched that LSU season and doesn't think the Burrow family fully grasped what Joe means to this state.

"They're gonna put a fucking statue outside of Tiger Stadium of this kid," he told Joe's brother Dan. "He's on the Mount Rushmore. You don't realize. He will never have to pay for a meal or drink in this state ever again."

So as the Bengals have gone on this shocking run, Hebert starts every Monday talking more about Burrow on his ESPN morning radio show, "Off The Bench". It's all anybody wants to talk about. He playfully compares himself to John the Baptist preaching Burrow's glory.

"Immortality that can be gained by accomplishing some of these things. So even though it's been two years, and maybe because of how the last two years have gone for LSU, Joe Burrow's star has not been lessened in the slightest. It's only been heightened."

—————— ——————

After watching Burrow and the Bengals clinch a trip to the Super Bowl, Kyle Schwarber can really relate to Chicagoans.

"Cubs fans might feel like I'm being a little outrageous here, but I know what it feels like to be a fan in '16 now," said Schwarber, a Middletown, Ohio, native and lifelong Bengals fan.

Schwarber, who helped lead the Cubs to a historic World Series championship, watched the Bengals rally from an 18-point deficit against the Chiefs in the AFC Championship at the new house he and his wife had just built in Middletown. How excited was he? Well, when asked if he were wearing a jersey for the game, this was his answer:

"Well, I've got a rotation," he said. "I got a (Joe) Mixon, I got a Tee Higgins and I got a Burrow jersey. So sometimes I rotate them out between quarters, things like that. Just try to change up the mojo. Last week, I started with the Tee Higgins jersey and once we got to that second half, I said, 'Yo, we got to switch up the mojo' and I put the Joey B jersey on."

Schwarber, who is a free agent waiting for the MLB lockout to end, procured four tickets to the Super Bowl. He stressed how the experience alone could benefit Burrow and the young Bengals in the future. Schwarber has experience in professional locker rooms and has played with renowned leaders like Jon Lester. He sees something special in Burrow, if only from afar.

"I think the biggest thing when you look at this guy talk, is he talks about his teammates a lot," he said. "He doesn't really talk about himself. I think that that's a special thing that you see. Obviously, he's the quarterback of the team, he's going to be making a lot of decisions, but he trusts his teammates. He trusts that they're gonna do the right thing for him to get the ball to them. And they're gonna make the plays. He believes in his team, and his team believes in him. That's half the battle. Now, it's just go out there and do it."

Schwarber is onto something with his assessment of Burrow, according to one of his former teammates.

"I've never seen him rattled," said Williams, Burrow's running back who went on to play at Northwestern. "I've known him since I was 15. Not one situation has he ever been rattled. That's just not in his DNA. And people gravitate toward that, whether it's fans, whether it's people on the same team as him. And I mean, in my experience, being on the same team as him, you don't want to let somebody like that down."

As a sports town, Cincinnati has needed someone like Burrow for a long time.

As the starting quarterback for the University of Cincinnati in 2008-09, Tony Pike led the team to two BCS games. Now he hosts a sports-radio show in the city and is basking in the glow like everyone else.

"Everyone's sold out of Bengals stuff and everyone you see is yelling, 'Who Dey,'" he said. "It's amazing what winning and sports can do for a frickin' city."

Pike grew up there, so he's familiar with the downside of being a local fan.

"You grow up in Cincinnati and all you really know is heartbreak," he said.

There's Jeremy Hill's playoff fumble against the Steelers six years ago, and a decade before that, Steelers lineman Kimo von Oelhoffen tumbling into Bengals quarterback Carson Palmer's knee. Kenyon Martin getting injured before the NCAA tournament in 2000. The Bengals' two Super Bowl losses in the 1980s. On and on. The Reds' 1990 World Series was a long time ago.

"It's always that tugging feeling as a Cincinnati sports fan of, you know, you're going to get pulled back down to reality," Pike said. "And you're going to face this heartbreak and all of a sudden here are the Bengals."

And here is Joe Burrow.

"There's the side of playing the game that I look at Joe Burrow, and I say, you know, he got drafted two years ago, he had a virtual offseason because of COVID," Pike said. "He gets major knee reconstructive surgery in his second offseason. So he's not had one normal offseason. He's not had the normal progression that every quarterback coming out of college gets. And I think you could talk about him as a top-five quarterback in the NFL right now. So there's that side of Joe Burrow.

"And then there's the Joe Burrow that literally has the city in the palm of his hands, right? He wears the Cartier glasses, and everyone goes and buys the glasses. And he wears the chain. And everyone's talking about that. Everything that he does is front-page news in the city of Cincinnati, and he does it without being like the boisterous over-the-top talker, right? He's one of those guys that is quiet. When he talks, you listen. But whatever he does, people are wrapped around what he does."

At Cincy Shirts, a top producer of local zeitgeist sports and culture apparel, they're working seven days a week to fill orders for Bengals gear for the Super Bowl. During the playoffs, its top seller has been the "Joey Warhol" shirt, a pop-art creation celebrating Burrow rocking those Cartier "buffs" to the press conference following the Bengals' first playoff victory in 31 years.

"Speaking as both a business owner and a fan, we haven't seen the total package, you know what I mean?" Sneed said. "We've lacked a guy that has that swagger that it's just teetering on the borderline of confidence and cockiness, but also the skill to back it up where you have the confidence in him to come through. We've just needed that guy."

---------------- ----------------

For the second time in three years, Burrow finds himself on the biggest stage he's ever been on, and on the cusp of doing something nobody expected. During this ride that has taken him from Athens to Columbus to Baton Rouge to Cincinnati and now to Los Angeles for the biggest game of his life, everyone around him says Joe Burrow hasn't changed a bit.

But those places he's been? Well, he's changed everything. ▬▬

Changing the Game

The Reinvention of the Bengals Continues Under Joe Burrow

By Paul Dehner Jr.

MARCH 14, 2022

Imagine a world where the Cincinnati Bengals, fresh off an AFC Championship, lead off the action mere minutes into the legal tampering period of free agency by dropping nearly $10 million per year on an offensive guard.

No, really, think about that sentence.

Imagine repeating it to your friends three years ago.

Add it to the list of ways Joe Burrow has changed every aspect of this franchise.

The franchise that would at one point rather polar bear plunge off the Brent Spence Bridge into the Ohio River than participate in the first wave of free agency took four minutes past noon for an Adam Schefter tweet to inject life — and Alex Cappa — into the Cincinnati fan base.

The franchise that shipped Max Montoya, Eric Steinbach, Kevin Zeitler and every other guard of prominence into the free-agent abyss at the moment of needing to pay near the top of the market, decided to drop four years and $35 million on the former Buccaneers right guard. They then followed it up hours later dropping $18 million on interior lineman Ted Karras.

The reinvention of the Bengals continues.

It used to be true Bengals fans never could enjoy all the fun parts of the NFL. Active offseasons, postseason victories, elite quarterbacks. Now they check off every box for a rejuvenated fan base soaking up — and literally buying in on — every moment of it.

Every move comes with Burrow's knee, throat, pinky and, most importantly, mindset at the forefront of decision-making. When it became obvious the team needed to provide a better pocket on the interior for him to work his magic, the Bengals listened and acted with purpose in bagging Cappa and Karras.

The highest average annual value paid for a guard in team history was $5 million per year for Clint Boling. They doubled that four minutes into free agency. Forget decades of Band-Aids and draft picks trying to fill the role inside, it was time to invest. The quarterback needed a change of philosophy and the Bengals provided it.

Yeah, the Super Bowl run was impressive, but if Burrow can make the Bengals' front office care about guards, he really can do anything.

They also did it in a way on brand with the type of player Burrow, head coach Zac Taylor and the front office prefer.

Cappa didn't allow a single sack in 2020. He comes with the reputation for glass-eating that offensive line coach Frank Pollack is chasing and a physical pass protector who can hold the pocket at a consistent level.

Of 85 qualifying guards last season, Karras ranked seventh in pass-blocking grade by Pro Football Focus and Cappa 29th. In true pass sets, Karras graded out as third and Cappa 34th.
Cappa is 27 years old. Karras turns 29 on Tuesday.

They each topped 3,000 snaps over the course of the last three seasons, giving up a total of 16 sacks during that time. For perspective, last year alone, Quinton Spain and Hakeem Adeniji combined to give up 16 sacks.

Burrow needs a protected pocket. The Bengals found reliable, consistent pocket protectors.

Karras will slot as the starting center but has played at a quality level at both interior positions.

In the no-donkeys quest to find at least average play at every position, Karras is the perfect example. He doesn't break the bank, brings consistency and reliability and can move to another spot should injuries or personnel dictate.

But this wasn't just about instant and aggressive addressing of offensive line instead of half-measures and draft pick development. This was about continuing to build a team of players defined by toughness, love of the game and physicality.

Cappa once tried to play in a playoff game against Washington with a broken leg. Karras was noted by defensive lineman Matthew Judon as embodying their desired physicality up front. Bill Belichick raved about the consistency of effort received from Karras every day of the week.

These are the types of characteristics and stories heard on repeat over the course of the Bengals' playoff run when questions were asked as to why this team overachieved and why they all seemed to get along so well.

They sought more of those characteristics up front. Pollack made it a search for "glass-eaters" and "alpha males." These two came with that reputation.

They also come with rings.

Both won the Super Bowl protecting for Tom Brady. Cappa in 2020, the year he didn't give up a sack, and Karras in 2016 and 2018.

By signing Cappa and Karras at reasonable deals, it leaves the door open for more. In terms of actual 2022 cap hit, Cappa will account for $6.8 million and Karras $5 million.

And to think, this was lining up to be much more. Coincidentally, it all ties back in with Brady.

The cannonball of the weekend washed a ripple effect over the Bengals when Brady announced he was returning to Tampa Bay. One of his first orders of business was to ensure center Ryan Jensen

came back to the Bucs with him. Jensen did agree to re-sign for three years and $39 million.

Jensen was the Bengals' top target entering the week and they held a belief they would end up with him and Cappa side-by-side. Director of player personnel Duke Tobin said at the NFL Scouting Combine if he was going to spend big money on a free agent — and specifically a free-agent offensive lineman — "it better be worth it." They felt Jensen would be.

Then the GOAT came back. Plans change.

Free agency is always a roller coaster and one that makes it entertaining for fans, but often nauseating for teams. Then you throw in a surprise shockwave like Brady and unpredictability reigns supreme.

Due to the way these chips fell, however, the Bengals can turn attention to Cowboys tackle La'el Collins, an addition that would execute a finishing move on the offensive line rebuild on par with Kano in the old Mortal Kombat video game ripping the heart out of his opponent and holding it in the air.

Collins has been made available for trade, but the Cowboys have not found any takers as they try to unload his salary before the start of the new league year Wednesday. Collins missed all of 2020 with a hip injury that required surgery and did serve a five-game suspension for violating the substance abuse policy last year.

Those red flags and knowledge that the Cowboys are just going to release Collins if a trade doesn't happen have hampered his value. Signs are pointing increasingly toward his release Wednesday.

It would be easy to think a player like Collins, who is only 28 and widely viewed as a top-10 right tackle in the NFL, should be in higher demand and warrant a huge contract. The lack of takers on the trade is surprising but also suggests he won't get rich. Where would that figure end up if he was released? The Bengals are expected to be involved, as they have been the entire time. Collins has a direct connection with Pollack, who coached him during his early seasons in Dallas. But the unpredictability of what it will cost to land him makes it one of the most unique final chips in free agency.

If the Bengals could find a way to make Collins happen, the liability of last season's line would seem to suddenly morph into a strength.

Consider the PFF rank of the players who finished last year on the line for Cincinnati:

LT: Jonah Williams (31 of 88)
LG: Quinton Spain (44 of 88)
C: Trey Hopkins (36 of 40)
RG: Hakeem Adeniji (85 of 88)
RT: Isaiah Prince (86 of 88)

It could turn into this in 2022, with only one bet on the development of two draft picks from last year:

LT: Jonah Williams (31 of 88)
LG: Jackson Carman/D'Ante Smith/Free agent (?)
C: Ted Karras (15 of 88)
RG: Alex Cappa (18 of 88)
RT: La'el Collins (15 of 88)

Other options could emerge to play right tackle if Collins doesn't end up in Cincinnati. The likes of veterans Morgan Moses (Jets) and recently released Daryl Williams (Bills) would fit the plan. Maybe Riley Reiff opts to stick around and finds a price that fits both sides. Or Smith could be given a real chance to take over the position in a battle with Prince, hoping one of the two finds themselves with another offseason to take a step.

All of that hangs in the balance of what unfolds over the course of the rest of the week. But those are sizzle options to consider because the Bengals took care of the steak immediately Monday.

Secure the middle, protect Burrow's pocket, keep him happy, keep him upright and enjoy what comes next.

The Bengals spent the money, found the fits and paid what needed to be paid. Coming off two offseasons where they combined for the fourth-most money spent in free agency, the fun has become a habit in March. Free agency used to be reserved for complaining about ownership and sending memes about how the team never does anything.

Monday was the latest example those days are gone. Or maybe the angst just moved to the stadium down the street.

Either way, in Cincinnati, The Burrow Effect rolls on. ■■■

Breaking Through

Joe Burrow Joins Josh Allen and Justin Herbert in QB Tier 1 Debut

By Mike Sando

JULY 25, 2022

I t's a new era for Quarterback Tiers as 50 NFL coaches and executives have shaken up the elite ranks for 2022, the ninth incarnation of my annual survey.

Young guns Josh Allen, Justin Herbert and Joe Burrow have joined the Tier 1 ranks, while a couple big names are conspicuously missing — including a certain quarterback the Seattle Seahawks traded to the Denver Broncos in a blockbuster deal recasting expectations for both franchises.

The full 2022 Quarterback Tiers results are below for every veteran starter. The results reflect voting from 50 NFL coaches and executives, including six general managers, eight head coaches, 10 evaluators, 12 coordinators, six quarterback coaches and seven execs whose specialties include analytics, game management and the salary cap. The remaining ballot was put together by four members of one team's personnel department.

The panel placed 35 veteran quarterbacks into one of five tiers, from best (Tier 1) to worst (Tier 5). Quarterbacks were then ranked by average vote and placed into tiers based on vote distribution, beginning with Aaron Rodgers, whose 1.00 average vote reflected his status as a unanimous Tier 1 selection.

The survey excludes rookies because voters have not seen them play in the NFL. More than one quarterback is featured for teams with unsettled starting jobs.

TIER 1

A Tier 1 quarterback can carry his team each week. The team wins because of him. He expertly handles pure passing situations. He has no real holes in his game.

1. Aaron Rodgers
2. Patrick Mahomes
3. Tom Brady
4. Josh Allen
5. Justin Herbert
6. Joe Burrow

Burrow has started 26 regular-season games and four in the playoffs. He has made it through one season healthy. He also quarterbacked the Cincinnati Bengals to the Super Bowl after Vegas set Cincy's win total at 6.5, fifth-lowest in the league. Voters love how he plays.

"Burrow is a young Tom Brady," said a GM who placed Allen and Burrow in the top tier, but not Herbert. "I think Herbert has shown he can do it in doses. Burrow is a step ahead. I think his mind is a lot quicker than Herbert's. Burrow wins with his brain, and he has had to, because he played behind probably the worst offensive line ever to go to the Super Bowl."

Burrow's accuracy, calm under pressure and willingness to stand strong in the pocket even when he's taking punishment has earned admirers.

"This league is in good hands with the quarterbacks right now, and they're in good places, with (coaches) who like to throw the ball," a head coach said. "These veteran guys know that these colleges are throwing the ball more and they had better maximize their abilities, man, or they ain't going to be doing it long, because the colleges are putting out better guys right now."

Any concerns on Burrow?

"He got fooled on that fourth down in the Super Bowl," a quarterbacks coach said. "He predetermines a lot of his quick game. They'll spread it out and try to show him the picture. When you can change the look for him, I think the kid locks in and some of these guys. Once you get a book on them a little bit, you can make these guys struggle a little. I'm not saying this is a guy you are going to take off the map. The kid is a competitor. I'm just saying he clearly predetermines some things and until he grows out of that, he is a good 2 for me."

A head coach who placed Burrow in Tier 1 explained that Burrow's poor offensive line was a contributing factor.

"Joe reminds me of the West Coast Offense quarterbacks you always were looking for with the anticipation, instincts, ball accuracy, throwing guys open," another head coach said. "You just don't see that at a very young age coming out, and I'm talking particularly from the drop-back phase. I'm a Joe Burrow fan. I'd put a 1 on him." ▬▬

What's Next for Joe Burrow?

Bengals' Star QB Poised to Join NFL's Greats

By Paul Dehner Jr.

AUGUST 1, 2022

At the start of Bengals training camp a year ago, the questions about Joe Burrow were as numerous as the potential range of outcomes.

Would he prove worthy of the first pick? Would he finish the season healthy? Could he make a leap in production after returning from a ravaged ACL? And how would the view of Cincinnati's future change if he didn't?

Burrow spent the next seven months laying waste to any questions about his career arc.

Like few things in sports and life, Burrow lived up to the hype. Joey Franchise proved to be the elite quarterback organizations dream about. In two seasons, he has erased a 31-year playoff-win drought and returned the Bengals to the Super Bowl for the third time in the 54-year history of the club. Stardom arrived.

He finished as an MVP candidate and the comeback player of the year, and combining the regular season and the postseason, he was Pro Football Focus' top-graded quarterback. He shrugged off 70 sacks, an ACL recovery, a throat contusion, an MCL sprain, a dislocated pinky and an ankle injury to will the Bengals to an 8-3 record after the bye week in games he started. That included a win at the No. 1-seeded Titans and two against Patrick Mahomes and the Chiefs.

He transformed the Bengals' culture, expectations and entire brand. His extreme confidence and humble work ethic permeated and defined an often rudderless franchise and reactivated a disconnected fan base. Not a bad encore after posting arguably the greatest season in college football history while winning a national title at LSU.

"He's everything you would wish for," Bengals president Mike Brown said, "especially for a quarterback in Cincinnati."

The primary question surrounding the 25-year-old quarterback a year later: What can he possibly do next?

———————— 𝔸 ————————

To understand where Burrow could go in his third season and beyond, we must fully understand where he's been — and the rare company he joined in the process.

Last summer, in advance of Burrow's second season, I took a deep look at the history of the second-year jump for quarterbacks over the past 15 years. The parameters were at least 350 passes thrown in the first and second seasons. The metric used was adjusted net yards per attempt-plus (ANY/A+). The stat takes the important yards-per-attempt number and weights for touchdowns and interceptions. To account for era, the scale is based on 100 being the average score for a quarterback in a particular season. So, if a quarterback scored 109, he was 9 percent better than the average quarterback that year. If he scored 91, he was 9 percent worse than the average quarterback that season.

Countless metrics, advanced and traditional, are used in evaluating NFL quarterbacks. Using ANY/A+ was an intentional choice as it is one of the metrics most correlated to winning, as exhaustively researched by The Michigan Football Analytics Society.

ANY/A+ of the past 12 Super Bowl QBs

YEAR	TEAM	SUPER BOWL QBS	ANY/A+ (RANK)
2021	Rams	Matt Stafford	116 (3)
2021	Bengals	Joe Burrow	116 (2)
2020	Bucs	Tom Brady	116 (7)
2020	Chiefs	Patrick Mahomes	127 (2)
2019	Chiefs	Patrick Mahomes	127 (1)
2019	49ers	Jimmy Garoppolo	112 (8)
2018	Patriots	Tom Brady	115 (6)
2018	Rams	Jared Goff	120 (5)
2017	Eagles	Carson Wentz*	117 (6)
2017	Patriots	Tom Brady	119 (4)
2016	Patriots	Tom Brady	138 (2)
2016	Falcons	Matt Ryan	141 (1)

A team with a quarterback outside the top quarter of the league in ANY/A+ has no chance. Every Super Bowl quarterback ranked in the top eight of the league, with half of them in the top three. Efficiency, explosiveness, limiting turnovers and cashing in on red zone opportunities define wins and losses.

Burrow made a jump from 93 as a rookie to 116 last season. That tied his Super Bowl foe, Matt Stafford, for second in the league behind Aaron Rodgers. Burrow's 23-point jump from his first to his second season was the largest made by a qualifying quarterback since Carson Palmer went up 26 points from 2004 to '05.

(Note: A quarterback's first season taking substantial snaps is used as the first year, regardless of the draft year; hence, Palmer's first season counting as 2004. Same for Mahomes, whose season behind Alex Smith did not count in this study.)

The numbers are backed up by the evaluators. In the latest QB Tiers by the The Athletic's Mike Sando, Burrow elevated to a Tier 1 quarterback for the first time. His move from 14th overall (Tier 2) to sixth in this year's edition was the largest leap for any quarterback.

Toss in Burrow's leadership and unwavering performances in last season's most critical moments while helping the Bengals advance to the Super Bowl, and there's no debating whether he belongs in the conversation with the best in the game. The questions: What comes next? What do we know about his ability to stay there?

The answers require a look back at ANY/A+. Only nine quarterbacks in the past 30 years have posted an ANY/A+ of at least 115 in their second season. So what happened next with that group? What are the odds of a fall from grace? How did their careers advance after the dominant second season?

Here's the group of quarterbacks and their ANY/A+ for the next three seasons, including the number of seasons in which they posted at least 110:

Career arc of QBs with 115+ ANY/A+ in Year 2

PLAYER	YEAR 2	YEAR 3	YEAR 4	YEAR 5	110+ CAREER
Patrick Mahomes	127**	127*	111	N/A	4/4
Kurt Warner	137	130*	INJ	INJ	6/9
Lamar Jackson	125	106	94	N/A	1/4
Jared Goff	121	120*	102	100	2/6
Carson Palmer	121	117	108	INJ	4/11
Peyton Manning	120	127	109	113	13/17
Carson Wentz	117**	110	100	71	2/6
Joe Burrow	116*	N/A	N/A	N/A	1/2
Russell Wilson	115**	109*	123	106	6/10

**Won Super Bowl   *Lost Super Bowl

There are no guarantees of holding the same high level of play in the long run; however, almost across the board, Year 3 has served as a continuation of the successful second year. Of the eight quarterbacks before Burrow to post this number, a whopping four went to the Super Bowl the next season. And two of them — Mahomes and Russell Wilson — returned after making it the previous year.

Sample-size concerns are noted, but the correlation is remarkable.

Beyond Year 3, the depreciation and lack of consistency in the group start to show up. Some, such as Carson Wentz, Jared Goff and Palmer, fell off. Others battled injury. A select few, such as Peyton Manning, Kurt Warner and Mahomes, sustained Hall of Fame trajectories.

The years after Burrow's anticipated record-breaking contract is signed and starts to dominate the Bengals' balance sheet will determine the group with which he ultimately winds up. But for the sake of the upcoming season, judging off the arc of similar performers, Cincinnati should prepare for another fun ride on Burrow's rising star.

Comparisons across generations happen all the time in the NFL, but never more than with quarterbacks. With Burrow, one name repeatedly surfaces.

"Burrow is a young Tom Brady," one NFL general manager said in Sando's QB Tiers.

As much as the style of play, leadership savvy and underdog backstory through the college ranks connect him, the name on the ANY/A+ list worth emulating is another used around Burrow inside the Bengals organization: Peyton Manning. Offensive coordinator Brian Callahan was an offensive assistant on the Broncos staff with Manning for four years, advancing to two Super Bowls. He sees the traits that lifted Manning as the reason for potential with Burrow.

"To see that and a lot of similar traits in Joe when we first started the interview process, and see how he has developed his processes and what he thinks about football and how he sees it," Callahan said. "It's really beneficial to have been with Peyton because there are very few guys as good as him in preparing to play a position. That's something I've tried to impart on Joe and something where he's naturally that way as it is."

Don't expect the uber-competitive Burrow to be thinking about how Manning worked or Brady evolved while grinding through his journey to avenge a Super Bowl loss to the Rams. The key element for finding consistency, in his mind, means not being motivated by what others are doing.

"I don't think you can go as hard as you can every single day and think about someone else," Burrow said. "I think you have to think about what you need to do every single day and focus on getting better in certain aspects, whether it's getting stronger in the weight room and you hit a (personal record) on a lift or you're getting better technique or you have a breakthrough on the field as far as your mechanics. I don't go into my workouts every day thinking how I've got to outwork this guy. I've got to outwork myself from yesterday."

Head coach Zac Taylor says most days Burrow has already watched whatever he's about to show him for the game plan. For the man who keeps a chess board in front of his locker at all times, adjustments and scheme changes quickly make sense. Just as important, the high-level conversation that ensues, specifically for a player who is only 25, is where the consistency of play from week to week and — the Bengals hope — from year to year is grounded.

"He doesn't hesitate to ask questions and ask for further explanation — whereas some guys in the NFL will 'yes, sir' you to death that they understand when they really don't," Taylor said. "That's what's really good about him, is he'll give you the honest feedback you want."

Burrow and the Bengals were charmed last season. Tyler Boyd, Tee Higgins and Ja'Marr Chase played nearly every game. Evan McPherson made nearly every deep kick. The opponents were the most injured in all of football. The defense picked off eight passes in the playoffs to set up numerous short fields.

Taylor and Callahan say it's in seasons when the luck isn't so charming that Burrow can truly shine. His extreme preparation, in the mold of Manning, and leadership style, as a young version of Brady, can carry the franchise.

These comparisons are unfair entering just his third season, but Burrow's pace and impact make them improbably realistic.

"What great quarterbacks do is they make everyone around them better," Taylor said. "They get the most out of everyone else, whether everyone feels like the standard has been raised so that they feel like they have to match what he is doing because he is so prepared and hard working that we have to get to his level. At the same time, they can feel (it) not even with words but his demanding to 'Get on my level so we can keep doing this.' It doesn't have to be in words. It can be done just through actions. He's really special that way. That's probably how a lot of the great ones are."

Defenses won't play the Bengals the same this season. Burrow knows that. The coaching staff knows that.

Burrow completed 12 passes of at least 50 yards last season, the most of any season in league history dating to 1991, as far back as can be searched. Eight of those went for touchdowns.

To expect Burrow and the Bengals to sustain such a historic pace is unrealistic. Defenses shifted to more two-high shells to keep the passing game in front of them as the season progressed, and that will only grow this year. That's why Burrow has focused a specific part of his preparation for the upcoming season around growing a precision underneath passing game that can dissect teams on 10-play drives just as effectively as one long bomb.

"We just got to be more consistent, not rely on those big plays as much," Burrow said. "Teams are gonna be playing (Cover 2) and making us check the ball down and all that, so we gotta be able to sustain drives and run the ball and take what the defense gives us, all the way up and down the field, and then take those opportunities when they present themselves."

The Bengals will need to be significantly better at specific aspects of offense that dogged them at times last season, but they hope that much of that work is already done. Adding Alex Cappa, La'el

Collins and Ted Karras to the offensive line brings stability to the liability Burrow was often working around in 2021.

This will help improve on one of the worst short-yardage conversion rates in the league and sustain drives. But mostly it will be about taking the punishment off Burrow's body. Yes, the poor line contributed to the 70 sacks he endured during the regular season and postseason combined. But the next step for Burrow is a deeper understanding of how to limit punishment while not sacrificing spontaneous playmaking.

"The sack thing is legitimate, and there's some things that he can do to help that," Callahan said. "There's a time and a place to extend a play; there's a time and a place to throw the ball away or to take a checkdown or what have you. So it's hard to sit here and be like, 'Hey, this is exactly what you got to do.' Every down-and-distance is different, but there's moments where he could help take some of the heat off of himself and take a few hits off."

Burrow's style of play, though, is what put him on the list of the best second seasons in league history. The toughness displayed by taking nine sacks against Tennessee but standing up to deliver the game-winning bench route to Chase with the game on the line is what stands out to league executives ranking him as a Tier 1 quarterback.

He threw deep to C.J. Uzomah on fourth-and-inches in overtime of the opener to set up the victory. He audibled to take the hit against a zero blitz to win the game against Jacksonville, yelling, "You can't zero me!" all the way to the sideline. He threw behind Chase running the other direction in the end zone on fourth-and-5 against San Francisco. He converted third-and-27 to Chase against Kansas City to win the AFC North. The examples become too many to count.

They became almost ordinary. In many ways, for Burrow, it is.

"It's wanting to be the guy that has the ball in that situation," Bengals quarterbacks coach Dan Pitcher said. "A lot of guys say that because they know that is what they should say and that's what people want to hear. But there are very few guys who that is who they are. And that is who Joe is. He came to us that way. We are lucky to have him. I wouldn't trade him for anybody."

Burrow's toughness and belief have won over teammates at every stop and keep them wanting to stay on his level. Actions over words. For Burrow, it's as natural as it is intentional.

"As a quarterback, you're not playing the same game as everybody else on the field," he said. "You're back there, and it's more of a mental chess match than it is a physical toll on your body. So when you get a chance to show your toughness, I think as a quarterback, you have to. And that's popping up — and not having bad body language if you get hit — popping back up, getting back in the huddle and doing it again."

The concept defines Burrow on a micro and macro level: Pop up, get back in the huddle and do it again. Play after play, game after game, year after year.

"He's the toughest guy mentally I have ever been around," Pitcher said. "He's the most confident person I've ever been around."

Can Burrow be Brady? Can he be Manning, Rodgers or one of his heroes, Drew Brees? Or does this end up going the way of Goff and Wentz, who floundered and were dealt after early breakouts?

When dissecting the key to sustaining success, the difference between those who last and those who flash and fade is the mental aspect of the position. And what makes this staff believe.

"I don't think there is anything you can measure the key to sustaining success by," Callahan said. "I think it is how the quarterback is wired. What

is their mental makeup? Guys like Peyton, Brady, Brees, those guys are extreme, super tough, super dialed in and unbelievably driven. They don't allow themselves to fail.

"That's what makes Joe so much more of an impressive player, is his mindset. It's what's going to eventually transcend him and keep him in the top five like those guys." ▬▬

No part of this publication may be reproduced, stored in a retrieval system or transmitted in any form by any means, electronic, mechanical, photocopying or otherwise, without prior written permission of the publisher, Triumph Books LLC, 814 North Franklin Street; Chicago, Illinois 60610.

This book is available in quantity at special discounts for your group or organization.
For further information, contact:

Triumph Books LLC
814 North Franklin Street
Chicago, Illinois 60610
Phone: (312) 337-0747
www.triumphbooks.com

Printed in U.S.A.
ISBN: 978-1-63727-277-0

The Athletic

Paul Fichtenbaum, Chief Content Officer
Dan Kaufman, Editorial Director
Lisa Wilson, Editorial Director
Evan Parker, SVP/GM Content Operations
Daniel Uthman, Senior Managing Editor - Football
Dave Niinemets, Senior Editor – Football
Oscar Murillo, VP Design
Amy Cavenaile, Design Director
Wes McCabe, Lead Designer
Kenny Dorset, Head of Social Engagement
Trevor Gibbons, Partnerships Director
Casey Malone, Associate CRM Director
Amanda Ephrom, Brand Strategist
Tyler Sutton, Marketing Manager
Ryan Cole, Social & Programming Manager
Brooks Varni, Editorial Operations
Rosalie Pisano, Partnerships Manager
Emma Lingan, Programming Manager
Christy Aumer, Marketing Operations

Featured writers from The Athletic
Paul Dehner Jr., Jon Greenberg, Brody Miller, Jay Morrison, Mike Sando

Special thanks to the entire The Athletic NFL & College Football Staff

Content packaged by Mojo Media, Inc.
Joe Funk: Editor
Jason Hinman: Creative Director